INTERPRETING THE LANDSCAPE
from the air

One cannot understand the English landscape and enjoy it to the full, apprehend all its wonderful variety from region to region, without going back to the history that lies behind it.

William Hoskins, *The Making of the English Landscape*, 1955 p.13

INTERPRETING THE LANDSCAPE

from the air

MICK ASTON

TEMPUS

Cover illustrations:

Front cover landscape: *Gear, Cornwall*
Mick Aston portrait by Chris Bennett

Back cover insets (from left): *Stonehenge,*
Wiltshire; Cheddar Gorge, Somerset; Castle
Howard, Yorkshire

Back flap portrait of Mick Aston by Teresa Hall

To my patient pilots,
past, present and future

First published 2002

Published in the United Kingdom by:
Tempus Publishing Ltd
The Mill, Brimscombe Port
Stroud, Gloucestershire GL5 2QG

Published in the United States of America by:
Tempus Publishing Inc.
2 Cumberland Street
Charleston, SC 29401

British Library Cataloguing in Publication Data.
A catalogue record for this book is available from the British Library.

ISBN 0 7524 2520 X

Typesetting and origination by Tempus Publishing.
Printed in Great Britain by Midway Colour Print, Wiltshire

CONTENTS

ACKNOWLEDGEMENTS

My first debt is to the pilots who have flown me around various parts of Britain over the years. They have invariably been a cheerful and skilful lot and sometimes they have been able to get me to views of sites that have not been very easy for them. Mike Crimble, at the time a Hercules pilot with the RAF at Lyneham, in particular made himself and his Piper Colt aeroplane available for flights at almost any time so that we could take advantage of the weather and ground conditions. Steve Grand, before he became entirely engrossed in writing complicated computer games, took me on many memorable flights in his fixed-wing microlite from Westonzoyland in Somerset.

I am particularly grateful to the helicopter pilots on the flights for the *Time Team* programmes. Helicopters are in my opinion the best aircraft for air photography. Even though I think I understand the physics I still don't quite understand why they don't fall out of the sky. Every pilot tells me the same thing: they only stay up there because you believe that they will! At least with helicopters you can say 'back a bit', 'up a bit', 'stop' and so on and the pilot can make the machine do it.

PHOTO TERESA HALL

I am also grateful for the encouragement of my friends and colleagues who suggested I write this book. It is based not only on the flights carried out as part of making *Time Team* programmes, but also on the vast number of slides I had accumulated from other flights made over the last thirty years. I know that many of the people in the *Time Team Club* were also anxious that I should write such a book and I hope they find the result interesting and informative.

Over the years the producer, Tim Taylor, and the directors at *Time Team* have been very generous in allowing me to conduct most of the flights for the programmes. This has provided an unparalleled opportunity to see so many of the sites and landscapes of Britain from the air. The air view, to most people, is still a very unusual and unfamiliar view of their surroundings.

The staff at Tempus, unlike other publishers I have dealt with recently, have as usual been very helpful and accommodating during the preparation of this book. Thanks are due to Peter Kemmis Betty, Tim Clarke and Liz Rudderham. Thanks also to Chris Bennett for generously allowing the use of some of his superb pictures.

PHOTO CHRIS BENNETT

RIGGIN HILL

PHOTO TERESA HALL

As always it is a pleasure to acknowledge the continuing help and encouragement of my PA and research assistant, Teresa Hall, who has kept the rest of my complicated professional life going while I have indulged myself in the research and writing of this book.

INTRODUCTION

It is easily forgotten that the air view, from a small aeroplane with the doors or windows open, is still something that most people do not experience at first hand. The nearest they get to anything like this is perhaps to see the landscape that is familiar to them from an airliner, leaving for or returning from a holiday destination. Most of the time such aircraft fly far too high to see anything but the general outlines of a country.

We also forget that the air view has only been accessible for a very short length of time in human history. While balloons have been used to get aloft since the eighteenth century, both powered flight and photography were only successfully developed in the twentieth century. Accessible and reliable small aeroplanes and small portable camera equipment were only widely available for the last third of that century, and together with rising living standards and increasing amounts of disposable wealth, regular access to the air view is a relatively recent development. As with so much else, most of the improvements came about as a result of the Second World War. By 1945 aircraft and cameras had improved beyond all measure, aerial photography had become a standard technique of reconnaissance by the military, and many millions of aerial photographs had been taken which were to provide a unique record of the landscape of Britain in the middle of the twentieth century.

Along with this improvement in equipment went considerable development in the discipline of archaeology. While air photographs were being used to illustrate sites in the 1920s, this was clearly a novel idea then. The pictures in the early Royal Commission volumes for Wales for example are slightly fuzzy, do not show a great deal, are low-level bird's eye views, and were clearly included as a novelty because the view would be unfamiliar to most readers.

Between the wars, a number of pioneers began to realise the potential of the air photograph as a research tool. Major Allen took many photographs from his Piper aircraft of the Thames Valley showing extensive areas of cropmarks on the gravel terraces alongside the river. He also collaborated with O.G.S. Crawford, the first archaeologist with the Ordnance Survey, in a pioneer survey of Wessex from the air (1928) where, almost for the first time, photographs were analysed in detail to show how much more could be learned about the sites from the air view. A great deal of attention was given in their book to the landscape aspects of the subject.

After the end of the Second World War, Maurice Beresford was one of the first of the new generation of landscape scholars to begin to use the vast archive of RAF air pictures. These had been taken at the end of the war, between 1944 and 1948, and he used them for research into aspects of the historic landscape, in particular the extent and form of ridge and furrow and the identification of deserted medieval villages. The beginnings of the research into deserted medieval villages owed a lot to the study of these pictures, as it did to the work of another pioneer, Kenneth St Joseph at Cambridge. His pictures in particular, taken from RAF aircraft initially, began to show the potential of the technique in illuminating aspects of archaeology on the ground from the air. The use of low sunlight to highlight earthworks and light dustings of snow and frost to show differential melting over buried features came to be seen as very efficient ways of locating sites and of learning more about those already known. In particular the recording of vast areas of previously unknown, and therefore undocumented, cropmarks proceeded apace all through the 1960s and 1970s with the Royal Commission for England under the direction of John Hampton, building up another vast archive of air photographs.

William Hoskins had clarified the study of the historic landscape in 1955 with the publication of *The Making of the English Landscape*, making the memorable claim that 'the English landscape itself, to those who know how to read it aright, is the richest historical record we possess' (p.14). Subsequent decades saw the vigorous development of the study of the landscape by both archaeologists and historians. Fundamental to this research was the availability of aerial photographs of various types. Not only were the collections at Cambridge University and the various Royal Commissions on Historical Monuments for England, Scotland and Wales available, the latter including the RAF wartime vertical series, but a host of other agencies had air pictures taken. These ranged from local authorities and the Ordnance Survey to the pre-privatised statutory undertakers (water, gas and electricity) which increasingly were commissioning aerial surveys with photographs as part of their operations. In parallel the increasing availability of small aeroplanes to amateur pilots has meant that many archaeologists have had the opportunity to fly over their areas of interest and to record the features observed by photographic print or slide.

Though I first flew when I was about eleven, my own personal involvement began around 1971-2 when working on the Sites and Monuments Record for Oxfordshire County Council. In particular, I had to look at the sites that

Tiger Moth

might be affected by the construction of the M40 motorway between London and Oxford. Flying from Booker in Buckinghamshire in the front seat of a Tiger Moth aircraft, with the cockpit open to the elements, was a primitive and uncomfortable but exhilarating way to begin my air photography career. In addition it gave me the impression of what it must have been like in earlier days and made me feel like one of the pioneers. Very quickly I began to use the trips to record other features as well. Not only did I photograph particular prehistoric or early monuments but also towns and villages and distinctive areas of landscapes, such as the gravel terraces of the Thames valley, the wooded Chilterns and the open limestone uplands of the Cotswolds.

When I moved to Somerset as the first County Archaeological Officer in the county council (1974-8), I continued to use aerial photography as part of my examination of the Somerset sites and landscapes which I had to deal with. I flew in a Rallye Sport, not an ideal aircraft as it had a low wing and a fixed perspex canopy, with a rather deaf pilot who was an undertaker in his non-flying life.

Rallye Sport

I returned to Oxford to work in the External Studies Department of the university (1978-9), and the following year I went to work in Bristol University in the Extra-mural Studies Department. I then met, through another pilot, a Hercules (a military transport aircraft) pilot, who had his own mini-airforce, which significantly included a Piper Colt aircraft that was ideal for aerial photography. Over the next couple of years, with us both having very flexible job commitments, we flew all over Wiltshire, Somerset and Gloucestershire at every opportunity when there was good weather and flying conditions. Before flying with various helicopters for *Time Team* this was my most productive period of aerial photography.

During the period 1992 to the present I have mainly flown in helicopters, usually the ubiquitous Jet Rangers or the rather nicer Aerospatiale Squirrel helicopters, filming for television programmes. However, I have also flown in other aeroplanes during this period, notably an open fixed-wing microlite with the extremely low stalling speed of 25 miles per hour, carrying out surveys

over the parish of Shapwick in Somerset. I have made a series for HTV television, *Time Traveller*, and took part in a series, *History Hunters*, as well as taking part in over 100 *Time Team* programmes, and a number of special one-off programmes for Channel 4. This means I have probably looked at about 100 different landscapes from the air while filming. Some of what I have seen on these many trips over the last thirty years is described in this book.

If you are studying the development of the landscape in an area, almost any air photograph is likely to contain a useful piece of information. There are many sources of air photographs available to the researcher these days but the two most important national collections for England are housed at Cambridge and Swindon. The Cambridge Collection was built up by Professor St Joseph in the 1940s to 1960s and has large numbers of oblique or bird's eye views, particularly of earthwork sites. Many more pictures have been added in recent decades, including large areas of the country which have been recorded on vertical air

Piper Colt

Microlite

photographs – that is they look like maps. The address is: Cambridge University Department of Aerial Photography, The Mond Building, New Museum Site, Free School Lane, Cambridge, CB2 3RF.

The collection at Swindon, in the National Monuments Record, began as the air photograph collection of the English Royal Commission on Historical Monuments. This is now part of English Heritage. The equivalent air photograph collections for Wales and Scotland are still maintained by the respective Royal Commissions for those countries, rather than with the parallels to English Heritage, Cadw (Welsh Historic Monuments for Wales) and Historic Scotland. All these collections contain very large numbers of air pictures, particularly verticals. The addresses are as follows: NMRC, Kemble Drive, Swindon, SN2 2GZ; Royal Commission on the Ancient and Historic Monuments of Scotland, John Sinclair House, 16 Bernard Terrace, Edinburgh, EH8 9NX; Royal Commission on the Ancient and Historical Monuments of Wales, Crown Building Plas Crug, Aberystwyth, SY23 1NJ.

PHOTO CHRIS BENNETT

Bell Jet Ranger helicopter. Photo Chris Bennett

So why is aerial photography so useful to archaeologists, and in particular what can we see from the air which helps with our understanding of how the landscape developed? What can we expect to see on flights at different times of the year and how do features of interest to archaeologists and historians manifest themselves from the air? There are basically five sorts of features:

Earthworks

Earthworks appear as 'lumps and bumps' in the ground. Sometimes these are a reflection of the geology if there are buried strata of rocks, for example. But generally, as a result of erosion by rain and frost and so on, the landscape has been smoothed out over thousands of years of weathering. So any lump or hollow in the ground that is visible from the air, and of course on the ground, is likely to be

There are other collections held in local authority Sites and Monuments Records and with the electricity, water and gas companies, and the Ordnance Survey uses air pictures for updating its maps.

It is still a revelation to fly over an area that is the subject of some aspect of landscape research in a light aeroplane. It therefore follows that if you have access to a light aeroplane, then you will see the landscape from a very different point of view. You are likely to see features or the interrelationship of areas that had not occurred to you before.

It makes sense to take a camera with you to record what you see and to provide a record for your research. There are many good, relatively cheap and lightweight cameras available, and the quality of the film nowadays is generally very good. I have not used a digital camera so far, preferring single lens reflex cameras with zoom lenses. For years I used a Canon A1 fitted with a Vivitar 28-105mm Macro lens, but at present I am using the more automatic Pentax MZ 30 with a Tamron 28-300mm Macro lens.

With Stewart Ainsworth in a Jet Ranger – the usual Time Team *members in the helicopter.* Photo Chris Bennett

the result of someone modifying the surface of the landscape. Any ditches and pits that have been dug will silt up but not completely disappear. Any banks will remain even though they become severely worn down and collapse over time. When this is combined with the evidence for buildings collapsing and then becoming covered in vegetation and eventually a soil cover, it can be seen that earthworks will be one of the prime forms of surface evidence for buried archaeological features. Some earthworks are huge such as the banks of the defences of Iron Age hillforts and these have long been recognized, but other areas of earthworks are more subtle. After all it was many hundreds of years from the desertion of many medieval settlement sites until it was realised what their remains represented. Even less obvious earthwork sites than these are being found all the time: slight traces of prehistoric and medieval field systems, hardly detectable earthworks of prehistoric and native Romano-British settlements, and the remains of early industrial activity of all dates.

Even where there are good surviving areas of earthworks they will not be recognized as such from the air unless the lighting conditions are appropriate. Differential vegetation growth will often help as in figure 1 of ridge and furrow in Lincolnshire where the ridges have drier grass compared to that in the ditches where there is lush growth. In low sunlight the fronts of banks and ditches facing the sun will be highlighted whereas the sides facing away will be in deep shadow. From the air this pattern of highlights and shadows not only shows up areas of earthworks, which might just appear to be a flat field in normal light, but it also helps us to determine what sort of features are represented. Even large earthworks such as hillforts (2) are more obvious in such conditions. The defences of Barkston Heath hillfort in Lincolnshire stand out with the ramparts highlighted on one side and in shadow on the other. More typical of the earthworks encountered in any landscape research are those shown in figures 3 and 4. These represent one or more medieval

1 *Ridge and furrow earthworks at Normanton, Lincolnshire*

fishponds, with enclosure banks that probably had hedges on them once, areas of ridge and furrow and drainage ditches. None of these earthworks are more than a metre or so in height, and they probably all relate to agricultural activity over the last 7-800 years. Such features do not really constitute an archaeological site as such, but they are important components of the medieval landscape of this part of Herefordshire. These earthworks are typical of the low-key features that show us how the landscape was formerly organised and used. Air photographs taken in low sunlight add considerably to our understanding of what is going on in these fields. The orange and yellow circles, effects from the camera lens, show that the one picture was taken almost directly into the sun, the ideal angle to get the best shadows behind the earthworks. In the final example, of Basing House in Hampshire (5), low sunlight enables us to see the lower, less obvious earthworks of the gun platforms around the main earthworks of the circular castle, with its extensive foundations of brick sixteenth- and seventeenth-century buildings. The

13

2 *Barkston Heath hillfort, Lincolnshire*

and areas of medieval ridge and furrow. While this can be seen clearly on the ground, the full extent and the plan of the field system is more easily appreciated from the air.

Soilmarks

Soilmarks occur when features that existed up until recently as earthworks are ploughed. For some time the differences, for example, between the hard dry material of banks and the dark damp or wet material of ditches, will be readily apparent from the air. Over time these differences in colour will be blurred with repeated ploughings and the features will eventually disappear as the site or piece of historic landscape is destroyed. Features of all periods from very ancient to really quite modern will show up in this form. Several examples occur in this book but others are included here.

castle began as a ringwork and bailey castle of the Norman period and some of the more prominent earthworks relate to this phase of development.

In this book there are very many examples of good earthworks which have proved very useful to archaeologists in helping them to understand the sort of sites that once existed. In other cases the existence of earthworks combined with other sorts of evidence has enabled complex histories of the development of certain landscapes to be worked out.

Over both earthworks and cropmarks, during light dustings of snow or frost, differential melting can sometimes be observed. Slopes facing the sun or patches where the soil is slightly warmer will lose the snow or frost earlier and will show up with green grass from the air against the white of the rest of the field. Figure 6 shows this at Westbury sub Mendip in Somerset. Here on the south-facing slope of the Mendips the snow has melted enough to show up the extensive medieval strip lynchets

3 *Earthworks at Sutton, Herefordshire*

4 (Left) *Earthworks at Sutton, Herefordshire*

5 (Above) *Basing House, Hampshire – earthworks of the castle and the Civil War defences*

6 (Below) *Westbury sub Mendip, Somerset – differential melting of snow over medieval lynchets*

7 *Avebury Down, Wiltshire – soil marks of ring ditch, roads and early fields*

8 *Avebury Down, Wiltshire – soil marks of extensive rectilinear field system*

Figures **7** and **8** are two views of the area to the east of Avebury in Wiltshire. They show an area of soil marks, actually being ploughed as I flew over it, which represent an extensive area of a prehistoric and Roman landscape. The circular ring ditch of at least one possible barrow can be seen, together with a possible farmstead, a forked road and an extensive area of embanked fields. As this is an area of chalk the banks, built of chalk blocks, show up white, while ditches show as dark lines. Wetter patches and areas of deeper soil are brown and features that cross them are obscured.

At Frocester in Gloucestershire, Eddie Price has been digging a Roman villa with an earlier Iron Age farm and later, Anglo-Saxon, features. Following excavation the areas are backfilled and then ploughed over as part of the normal farming regime. Figure **9** shows the field ploughed with a later area of excavations in the middle. The villa and its outbuildings can be seen as areas of lighter soil, mixed with stone, in contrast to the generally stone-free clay areas of the rest of the field. By complete contrast, figure **10** shows a pattern of zig-zag patches along a road. As these are near the airfield at Kemble in Gloucestershire the context, which is always an essential consideration, is particularly relevant. It could probably be guessed that these are the ploughed out dispersal positions for aircraft around the airfield. Clearly the concrete has been removed and the plough is now cutting into the hardcore foundations.

Cropmarks

Cropmarks occur when ploughing has reduced earthworks to the level of the surface of the field and there is little if anything visible at ground level. While features may still show up as soil marks when the ground is being ploughed and prepared for sowing the crop, it is while the crop is growing that cropmarks appear. Generally they show up best with fine-grained crops such as cereals,

9 *Frocester, Gloucestershire – the area of the villa shows up as a lighter stony area to the left of the excavation*

10 *Kemble, Gloucestershire – soil marks at the ploughed airfield*

though they have been known to occur in other crops, including cabbages. They are formed as the crop comes under stress as it is growing usually from a lack of moisture or nutrients. The parts of the crop growing over buried ditches will tend to grow taller and remain greener longer as the crop ripens because they have a reserve of moisture and plant nutrients under them in the ditches. By contrast those areas of the crop growing over stony patches, such as the metalling of Roman roads or the walls of Roman villas, will tend to be stunted in their growth and ripen sooner than the bulk of the crop. This is because the plants are stressed with a lack of nutrients and moisture in the thin soil and the hard surfaces beneath their roots. In practice there must be all sorts of other reasons why crops

grow differently and ripen at different times within any particular field and we will probably never quite understand how different features are caused.

There are several examples in the landscapes discussed in this book but included here are some particularly interesting or informative examples. Figure **11** shows fairly typical cropmarks of what is probably a late prehistoric or Romano-British farmstead, although the actual house site is not showing up. A ditched road way running between two ditches, the dark lines (and probably originally between hedges) come up to series of ditched enclosures where the buildings of the farm were situated. Figure **12** is a similar example but here the crop is almost entirely ripe. The outline of a circular enclosure with slight traces of a

11 *Cropmarks at Sutton Benger, Wiltshire*

12 and **plan** *Cropmarks at North Petherton, Somerset*

round house inside it is approached by ditched roads. The ditches are just slightly greener than most of the crop but show up best because the picture was taken in low sunlight on a summer evening. Most of the features on this picture in fact are the result of the shadows from the slighter, higher areas of the crop which were growing over the enriched ditches. Incidentally there are two modern features on this picture which need to be understood if the earlier features are to be appreciated. One is the 'envelope' pattern, which is the result of modern ploughing techniques, and the other is the patches of flattened crop, where it is so ripe that it has blown over in the wind. The use of low sunlight throwing shadows behind slightly higher areas of crop can be seen very dramatically in figure **13**. Although it is not at all clear what sort of features are showing up here, they are probably field systems of different dates.

Rather clearer evidence of earlier ploughed out fields can be seen in figure **14** where the dark lines indicate the ditches (again probably originally accompanied by hedges) around the fields.

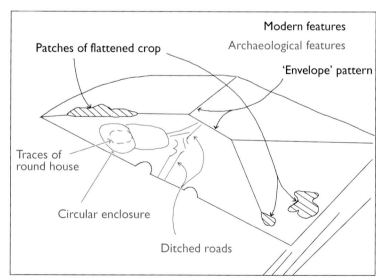

13 *North Petherton, Somerset – cropmarks of probable field systems*

15 and **plan** (below) *Foxley, Wiltshire – cropmarks of probable Anglo-Saxon buildings*

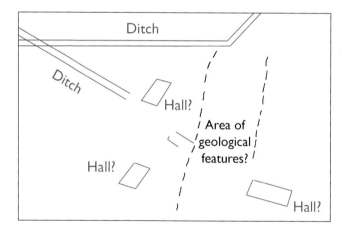

14 *Cropmarks near Preston St Mary, Suffolk*

Figure **15** is a very low level air photograph. The lines made by the tractors going through the crop can be clearly seen, and it is also just about possible to make out the individual lines of plants. Near to this field at Cowage Farm, Foxley, Wiltshire a complex of cropmarks was seen some years ago and after excavation was shown to be a 'palace' of the Anglo-Saxon period. Here across the stream from the 'palace' site there are rectangular cropmarks that seem to represent at least two more of the large rectangular buildings found on the main site. These were probably large timber-framed halls also dating from the Anglo-Saxon period. There are many other features here including lines (of ditches?), probable geological marks – which of course are common on these air pictures and have to be allowed for – and what look like pits showing up as dark blobs.

Parchmarks

Parchmarks are the equivalent of cropmarks but occur where there is grass rather than a crop growing over a site. In pasture areas of grassland where there are no earthworks and there has been no modern ploughing, it is often impossible to know whether there are any archaeological sites buried beneath. However, in times of drought the grass will wither and parch out over buried walls and stony areas. Often of course this can be seen on the ground or from a high vantage point such as a church tower, but some spectacular examples have been seen from the air. In this book, the example of the Roman villa at Turkdean in Gloucestershire showed up initially as parchmarks. As much as possible of the layout was recorded quickly on a plan since often a shower of rain will start the grass growing again and the marks, and details of the site, will then disappear.

During the research on the Shapwick project in Somerset parchmarks were frequently recorded. Shapwick parish is an area of the county with few earthworks and the local geology is mainly limestone. During dry periods and with only a thin covering of soil over the bedrock, which dried out quickly, parchmarks would appear indicating the underlying geological structure. Figure 16 shows the peculiar patterns which result, with curved lines of alternate parching and grass growth over rock and clay. Ironically there is a Roman village in the middle of this picture, which was later found by fieldwalking and geophysical survey, but the buried walls did

16 *Shapwick, Somerset – parchmarks of geological features*

not show up as parchmarks as these were too deeply buried in hillwash.

The earlier church site of Shapwick, which was out in the fields, has always been known by the villagers; it was moved into the village in the mid-fourteenth century. Figure 17 shows the early site along with many other features showing up in the grass. This is a permanent pasture field and has not been regularly ploughed since the sixteenth century so the marks are all showing up as differential grass growth. The darker areas are over ditches and deep areas of soil and show that the church was in an enclosure and that there was a spring alongside.

Parts of the village were removed in the late eighteenth century to create a small area of parkland in front of the main manor house (18). The alignment of the main road west of the village shows up as an earthwork with at least two side roads showing as parchmarks. A former road through the village, which was later cut by a ha-ha garden

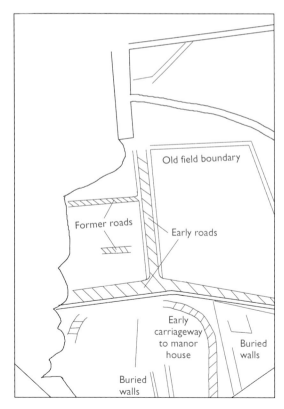

feature, is also apparent. In the foreground an earlier carriageway to the house together with even earlier walls associated with the monastic farm belonging to Glastonbury Abbey also show in the parched grass.

Patterns and alignments

Boundaries in the countryside and town and village properties are also a useful source of information and often make more sense from the air than on the ground, creating patterns and alignments that can be interpreted. Inhabited and built-up areas of houses, gardens, paddocks

17 Shapwick, Somerset – the early church site showing as parchmarks

Old field boundary

Former roads

Early roads

Early carriageway to manor house

Buried walls

Buried walls

*18 and **plan** Shapwick, Somerset – parchmarks of the roads and former village area in the park*

and so on can look very different from the air, even when compared to large-scale maps, and so patterns of boundaries and alignments may become of much more significance than had been noticed before.

It is difficult to define exactly how to interpret such patterns but a few 'rules of thumb' might help. Generally speaking there is a difference between regular areas of right-angled boundaries and alignments of hedges and properties, and those that appear to be more haphazard and chaotic in their arrangement. The former often look as if someone has laid out an area with surveying equipment, trying to get all the angles the same, such as ninety degrees. The others look like gradual or piecemeal activity resulting in a patchwork of boundaries and alignments as individual fields and plots are created.

Areas with regular patterns may indeed have been 'planned', or at least closely regulated by someone as they were being developed, and this is frequently what we deduce from such patterns. The less regular patterns may be the result of a more protracted period of creation with lots of stages of boundary development.

However, it may be going too far, with many patterns of boundaries, to think of 'planning' in the sense of the sort of activity which was undertaken at the time of enclosure of common fields and waste in many parts of the country in the eighteenth and nineteenth centuries. This resulted in the extremely regular rectangular patterns of field boundaries to be seen in many areas with long straight roads and tracks with wide verges. In the former medieval royal Forest of Neroche in Somerset, enclosure of what had been commons took place in the early nineteenth century (**19**). The surveyors planned a landscape of regular rectangular fields with long straight roads. The resulting landscape, viewed from the air over one hundred and fifty years later, looks like it was designed on a drawing board. By contrast figure **20** is a landscape on the edge of the Forest created as a result of 'assarting' (clearing trees) in the early Middle Ages and is much less regular. The fields cleared piecemeal out of the woods and waste are irregular in shape and size

with wiggly boundaries of thick hedges. Deep hollow lanes wander between the field banks and there are bits of uncleared woodland here and there.

Elsewhere long continuous boundaries or features, which are 'respected' or butted against by other boundaries, are generally assumed to be earlier in a sequence of development, though we usually don't have much idea of the time scale involved.

Finally something needs to be said of the pitfalls of using aerial photographs for archaeological work. Sometimes features are seen on air pictures that look convincing as previously unidentified archaeological sites. Mention has already been made of geological structures and some of these can look like patterns of early fields when they are in fact lines in the underlying bedrock resulting from periglacial conditions at the end of the last Ice Age. Modern agricultural practices can also deceive. The 'envelope' pattern seen in many fields has already been noted as well

19 (Opposite) *The Broadway area of the former Forest of Neroche, Somerset*

20 *The Dommet area of the former Forest of Neroche, Somerset*

as areas of blown-down crop. But leaky muck spreaders or sprinklers spreading liquid manure and producing circular patterns can also produce convincing 'archaeological' features. 'Fairy rings' are produced by fungi growing in the grass, and can look like the dark lines associated with prehistoric ring ditches from the air. It helps to know just what has gone on in recent years in the fields of an area if blunders of interpretation are to be avoided.

The pictures in this book and the places selected are only arranged in the roughest of chronological order. This is because in any area the landscape is a palimpsest of earlier periods all overlaid and combined. A palimpsest is an old parchment document that has been reused or a medieval memorial brass that has been turned over and reused, but it encapsulates the idea that the landscape is continually modified or totally erased by the next generation of farmers, quarrymen or whatever. Sometimes the slate was wiped completely clean and a totally new landscape was

laid out. Something like this happened on an enormous scale as a result of the Enclosure Acts in the eighteenth and nineteenth centuries when huge areas of countryside in the East Midlands were replanned and many of the uplands which had been open common pasture were walled in. But generally the landscape has evolved with constant adaptation and modification but few dramatic or drastic changes. Each generation has added and taken bits away so that most parts of the country are full of 'relict' features which make little sense now because they belonged to an earlier arrangement that did make sense. The bend in the road for no apparent reason, the change in hedge alignment, the strange circular arrangement of field boundaries is only intelligible if we can understand earlier patterns of which they are the remains. I hope something of the flavour of this comes out in this book.

The periods represented here range from the early prehistoric period with the Palaeolithic sites in Cheddar Gorge through to the modern period. There are a number of studies that are predominantly prehistoric, others that are Roman, and several that are mainly medieval. But in every case other periods are present as well and are relevant to what can be seen from the air. So the order of studies is only approximately chronological.

While there is much discussion here of sites and landscapes we can understand more of what we see on the air photographs perhaps if we see them as showing aspects of how early societies worked. I have found it useful over the years to see these landscapes as representing one of a number of themes. Clearly where people lived is fundamental – the settlements – whether they be towns and cities, villages and hamlets or farmsteads. These were surrounded by the different forms of land use from which the agricultural sustenance for the population was derived. These include the arable areas for crop growing, pasture areas for animals, meadowland alongside rivers and streams, and woodland for the production of wood and timber. The way these different land uses are organised can produce a variety of types of field system.

The links between the various settlements form the communication pattern. This will include major and minor roads with local lanes and paths, but also the canal, rail and turnpike road network and the use of rivers, estuaries and coastal sites. Within the landscape will also be those industrial and quarrying sites of all periods where those not engaged in agricultural activity worked often on a seasonal basis. While relatively little of this went on in the early periods it became increasingly significant from the seventeenth century onwards.

At all periods there were always some places in the landscape that were more important than others, and where special activities or functions were carried out. We can think of places today which have supermarkets, banks, building societies and solicitors' offices. Not everywhere has these and it was the same in the past. Some places were allowed to hold markets and fairs, where exchange of goods and services could take place. Some were the administrative and tax centres, others the focus of religious activity and

organization. From Roman times onwards we can think of the foci of these activities as the towns of Roman, medieval and modern times, though in the Anglo-Saxon period urban life seems to have declined and the same functions were carried out from rural centres. The same may be true for much of prehistory when towns in the modern sense do not seem to have existed. Some or all of these focal place activities probably took place at causewayed enclosures, henges, hillforts and so on.

One aspect, which is always well represented in any landscape, concerns the belief system of the people at the time. Ceremonial and burial monuments and sites, and those where ritual activity periodically took place, are usually significant centres, whether they are barrow cemeteries in the prehistoric period, or collections of monasteries, churches and a cathedral in a medieval city.

Finally there have been few times when defence of some sort has not been important, and consequently any landscape usually has defensive sites of one sort or another. These can range from the indeterminate linear ditch systems of later prehistory defining territories, through Roman forts, medieval castles and post-medieval gun platforms, to the vast range of military sites and structures dating from the two World Wars and the Cold War of the twentieth century.

When looking at any landscape from the air, some or all of these aspects will frequently be seen in the countryside below. The interrelationships between them at different periods, and the way they change over time, is what produces the different landscapes. Features left over from one period which then influence another are what give us the redundant or 'relict' boundaries, alignments or earthworks which are the clues to how any landscape has developed. The view from the air and air photography has proved one of the most powerful ways of beginning to understand much of what we see of the development of the landscape. I hope that this book will provide an interesting and informative introduction to what is one of the most fascinating aspects of modern archaeology in Britain.

1
CHEDDAR, SOMERSET

Cheddar has some claim to be one of the places that has been occupied the longest in the British Isles, some 13,000 years at least. This is based on the finds from the caves in the famous Cheddar Gorge, which include human skeletal material as well as bone and stone artefacts and tools. As we can see, the gorge leads down to the flat plain alongside the river Axe, and the present village and church is on this wider flatter area. In the background is the near circular reservoir built in the 1930s, and beyond the sea in Bridgwater Bay, and in the distance the Quantock Hills.

One of the most famous of the Cheddar caves, Gough's, can be seen in the bottom right of figure **22**. This has produced huge numbers of stone and bone artefacts of the palaeolithic or old stone age period, as well as the skeleton of 'Cheddar Man' and some controversial evidence of early cannibalism. This view also shows clearly how the gorge is a great cleft in the carboniferous limestone of the Mendip Hills. It is steeper on the right (east) side which was called Cheddar Cliff in earlier times. From this view it can also be appreciated why this feature was such an important area for prehistoric

21 *Cheddar Gorge, Somerset*

people hunting animals. The narrow gully of the Gorge meant that early prehistoric hunters could ambush herds of animals as they made their way from the lower flat plains of the Somerset Levels up to the higher grazing lands on top of the Mendips.

Ironically this hunting aspect was still important some 12,000 years later when the Anglo-Saxon kings of Wessex also hunted at Cheddar. Their palace was excavated (**23**) when the Kings of Wessex Community School was built in the 1960s. The large postholes were found which would have held the huge timbers put up to support the roof. The position of these posts has now been marked out with concrete blocks on the ground (though they are hardly visible in this air photograph). It is still difficult however to appreciate how large and magnificent these halls would have looked in the tenth to twelfth centuries when the royal site was at its most important. There is a later chapel on the site, dedicated to St Columbanus – its existence was a clue to the location of the palace, and there is a

22 *Cheddar Gorge with Gough's Cave bottom right*

23 *Cheddar – the site of the Anglo-Saxon palace at the school*

medieval manor house nearby. This was built by the four-teenth century after the palace was abandoned and probably forgotten.

The Anglo-Saxon palace did not exist in isolation and it did not represent the earliest occupation in this area of Cheddar (**24**). Neolithic material has been found not far from the church and there is probably a Roman villa under the lawn of the vicarage next to the church. There was also some sort of religious community here in the ninth and tenth centuries, though it is doubtful if it was ever a fully formed Anglo-Saxon monastery. We know little about this but it must be assumed that it was somewhere in the vicinity of the medieval church of St Andrew. Rather than being a royal Anglo-Saxon palace with an attached religious community, it is perhaps more likely that the religious site was used periodically by visiting royal groups who hunted locally and issued charters and so on from the timber halls on the site.

The villa, palace and monastery would not have existed in isolation in an empty landscape. There must have been settlements of farmers around supplying the dignitaries in the palace. Many of the present day farms can be shown by documents to be at least medieval in date so they are probably the successors of earlier Anglo-Saxon ones. One of these has been excavated at Carscliffe, high on the front edge of the Mendips, above Cheddar to which it was linked by a road, now abandoned as a holloway (**25**). Within the excavations are a number of buildings of medieval and later date; it looks as if the settlement was abandoned in the seventeenth and eighteenth centuries (**26**). There is enough tenth-century pottery from the excavations, however, to demonstrate that there must be a late Saxon farm in this area, which would have been contemporary with the palace. This and others must have produced the food and other materials consumed there.

Much of what can be seen in figure **24**, though, relates to the last three or four hundred years. The pattern of lanes and streets may well date back to the Anglo-Saxon and medieval periods (or even earlier), but the buildings,

24 *The Anglo-Saxon palace site at the school (left), the church of St Andrew (right) at the probable monastery site. Between is the site of the Roman villa*

25 *Carscliffe – excavations on the site of the Saxon and medieval farm*

26 *Carscliffe – the excavated buildings*

by and large, are all post-medieval in date. At the hub of the local village road system stands the late medieval 'cross', actually a small covered octagonal structure built to shelter traders, reminding us that Cheddar was a market centre. One of the commodities traded, which is of course world-famous, was cheese, produced from the milk from the many cows grazed on the lush summer pastures of the Somerset Levels to the south.

The Cheddar landscape therefore represents occupation and activity by people over a considerable period. They have lived, hunted and farmed here, and their leaders had important residences here. Not everywhere is as long-lived as Cheddar but much of the landscape is older and has been modified constantly over longer periods than we might initially think.

Further reading

Larry Barham, Philip Priestly & Adrian Targett, *In Search Of Cheddar Man,* Tempus Stroud 1999

Philip Rahtz, *The Saxon and Medieval Palaces at Cheddar*, British Archaeological Reports British Series 65 1979

2

THE STONEHENGE LANDSCAPE, WILTSHIRE

Stonehenge is undoubtedly the most famous prehistoric monument in the British Isles. But what is not so well known, except among archaeologists, is that it is only one site in a vast prehistoric landscape within which survive numerous other contemporary prehistoric monuments. Stonehenge is essentially a late Neolithic and early Bronze Age site, built, developed and altered over a time span of nearly two millennia or so, from around 3000 BC to nearly 1000 BC. The landscape around it is dominated by monuments that are roughly contemporary with it, including long and round barrows, other henge monuments and numerous other 'ritual' sites. We are probably justified in thinking of this as a prehistoric ritual landscape, for as we shall see all the monuments in it seem to be associated either with ritual or at least ceremonial activity and particularly with burial and celebration of the dead. Indeed one archaeologist, Michael Parker Pearson, sees Stonehenge as a monument of death, at the centre of a great burial landscape with concentric zones of groups of round barrows.

27 *The central area of Stonehenge*

There is little visible that indicates settlement and farming activity at the time the monuments were in use, and extensive field survey by Julian Richards and others has not really altered this picture. There is also very little visible that is later – there is little evidence for Iron Age and Roman monuments for example – and there is little evidence of medieval settlement in the vicinity. Field systems of small rectangular embanked closes, which may be later, do not impinge on any of the monuments, seeming to respect them in areas of pasture. Indeed the survival as earthworks of so many structures in the Stonehenge landscape is a powerful indicator of a lack of later disturbance by late prehistoric, Roman and medieval arable farmers. It seems likely that grazing with sheep must have been the traditional land use of the whole area for most of the last three thousand years.

Along with this remarkable survival of the prehistoric ritual landscape, we know a great deal about how it has changed in the past. Study of the past environments, based on such biological remains as molluscs, enables us to see an initially wooded countryside gradually being opened up by

28 *The bank and ditch around the stone settings at Stonehenge; the avenue is at the top out by the road*

several restoration projects to re-erect stones over the years, notably in the twentieth century. The sarsen stones were probably bought from somewhere on the chalklands locally where they occur naturally – the favoured candidate being the Marlborough Downs where the stones still occur in abundance, while the bluestones have been shown to come from the Preseli mountains area of Pembrokeshire in South Wales. This stone part of the monument, the most visible part today, was built from 2500 BC with alterations over the next thousand years.

But 500 years or so before the stones, the first phase of the monument was constructed – the bank and ditch around the site (**28**). There may have been a timber monument or building in the centre of this, there were certainly cremations, and the entrance may have been from the south.

Running away from the monument to the north-east is an earthen avenue, which eventually reaches the river Avon near Amesbury, though for most of its course it is ploughed out. This was presumably the main Bronze Age ceremonial way to the monument, and together with the configuration of the horseshoe-shaped settings within the circle suggests that people using the monument were looking to the south-west, both as they approached and when they were inside the circle. If the monument was related to alignments of the sun, this would suggest an interest in the setting of the sun in mid-winter, a critical time for farming communities since it marks the darkest time of the year after which the days get longer and it is clear that spring is on its way.

All around are other monuments. To the north is the 'cursus' (**29**), a long, lightly-banked enclosure over two kilometres long which dates to around 3000 BC. Even earlier than this are the numerous long barrows of the early Neolithic dating back to about 4000 BC. One of the most famous in the Stonehenge region is at the Winterbourne Stoke crossroads (**30**, **31**). This is a long mound with side ditches almost at the modern traffic island. It held burials and probably provided a focus for the local community,

tree felling and scrub clearance and then kept open as grassland by the grazing of animals. It is therefore likely that some of the monuments built in the Neolithic were within woodland, clearings or lightly wooded areas, whereas by the Bronze Age there was more open country. The generally very open landscape of today, predominantly arable and with numerous rectangular coppice woodlands and plantations, gives a distorted view of what the area was like when the monuments were built.

Stonehenge consists of a circle of sarsen stones with a circle of smaller 'bluestones' within it (**27**). Within that is a horseshoe-shaped setting of large sarsen stones mirrored again by a similar bluestone setting. This original scheme is now of course ruined and there have been

29 *The large cursus monument to the north of Stonehenge*

30 *Winterbourne Stoke crossroads barrow group with long barrow at the top by the road island*

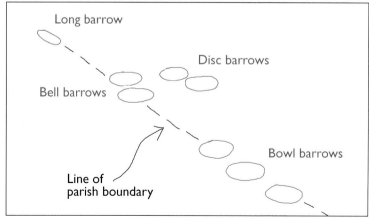

31 and plan *Winterbourne Stoke crossroads barrow group*

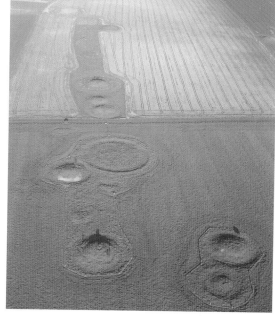

32, 33 *The Normanton Down barrow group to the south of Stonehenge; 'Bush' barrow has a tree on it*

rather like the parish church did in later times. At sites like Winterbourne Stoke can be seen a very large number of Bronze Age round barrows and indeed these are the most common type of monument in the Stonehenge region. Within the area of two to three kilometres diameter around Stonehenge there are several hundred of them, many very large and remarkably well preserved. Since they contain burials, usually a central primary one but also often subsidiary peripheral ones as well, Stonehenge seems to have been regarded as the focus for a vast necropolis landscape of particularly rich burials. For example the Normanton Down group (**32, 33**) includes several rare disc barrows and the famous 'Bush' barrow. This site produced a number of gold objects (which can be seen in Devizes Museum) probably indicating the burial of a chief sometime in the centuries either side of 2000 BC.

At Winterbourne Stoke there seems to be an example of every type of round barrow, from simple bowls to elaborate bell barrows, unusual disc barrows to enigmatic pond barrows. When excavated, some of these had wooded tree-trunk coffins and lots of finds of bronze daggers, beads and so on. These barrows were aligned on the long barrow and this alignment persisted in the landscape as a Saxon boundary, a time when more peripheral burials were put

into these mounds, and it is still a parish boundary today. The layout of the long barrow in 4000 BC determined the line of the Bronze Age barrow cemetery a thousand years later. In turn this was used as a territorial boundary nearly three thousand years later in the Anglo-Saxon period (if indeed it had not been a boundary continuously for all that time) and which is still a local administrative unit boundary today – the civil parish. Some of the oldest and most persistent features in the landscape turn out to be not monumental structures, but the layout and orientation of such slight features, possibly not even marked on the ground, as property and administrative boundaries.

Further reading

Julian Richards, *The Stonehenge Environs Project*, English Heritage 1990

Julian Richards, *Stonehenge*, Batsford English Heritage 1991

Ann Woodward, *British Barrows: A Matter of Life and Death*, Tempus Stroud 2002

3

THE AVEBURY LANDSCAPE, WILTSHIRE

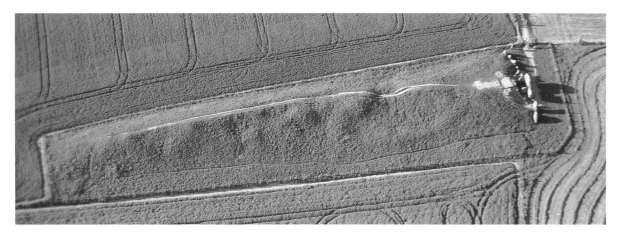

34 *The West Kennet long barrow*

Other than the Stonehenge region, the Avebury area is one of the richest landscapes for seeing monuments of the early prehistoric period still intact. The great henge monument with its circles of huge stones is, like Stonehenge, merely one of a large number of monuments scattered over the landscape. Rather like Stonehenge these have more to do with ritual, ceremonial and burial activity than settlement and farming, though unlike the Stonehenge landscape there is more evidence for later prehistoric, Roman and medieval settlement activity including a village within the Avebury circle itself. Also like the Stonehenge region we know a certain amount about the natural landscape of the area which we now know changed from predominantly forested to more open countryside as time went on.

The earliest monuments in the landscape date to the early Neolithic period and include many long barrows and several 'causewayed' enclosures. The most famous long barrow is at West Kennet where a huge long mound over 100m in length (**34**) covers a stone-built burial chamber in the east end (**35**). Remains of over 40 individuals were buried over a period, before the tomb was blocked. This occurred at the beginning of the Bronze Age when the tomb was filled with soil and the entrance blocked by larger stones. We know about this because the site was excavated in 1955-6. Rather more typical in terms of surviving appearance is the long barrow at Adam's Grave (**36**) to the south of Avebury built on a prominent hill overlooking the Vale of Pewsey. Despite recent local quarrying, the prominent long mound is still impressive

35 *The stone burial chambers at the east end of the West Kennet long barrow*

36 *Adam's Grave long barrow from the north*

37 *Windmill Hill causewayed enclosure with Bronze Age barrows*

with a hollow at the east end where the burial chamber probably is, and the side ditches from where the material of the mound was excavated. This barrow was called 'Wodenesbeorg' or Woden's Grave in Saxon times and was the focus of two battles, fought in 592 and 715.

The contemporary or slightly earlier 'causewayed' enclosures seem to have been seasonally occupied settlements or meeting places – perhaps a sort of fair place where groups met up periodically to exchange goods, people and news. They consist of a series of concentric

lines of ditches interrupted with areas of rock left unquarried (hence 'causeways') enabling access to the interior. There were banks inside the ditches. The 'type-site' is Windmill Hill north of Avebury, which has been excavated and partly restored (37). A rather better preserved site where the causeways can still be clearly seen is Knap Hill (38) well to the south of Avebury and close to Adam's Grave. Off one end of this site are the earthworks of a Romano-British farmstead. Because of the undisturbed nature of the downland here a number of earthworks of different date survive intact (39).

Avebury itself consists of the circular earthworks of the henge monument, consisting of the deep interior ditch and the huge outer bank. In places there is a flat space between them, which was probably formerly more extensive, called the berm. On the inner edge of the inside platform were erected large sarsen stones, probably derived from the nearby Marlborough Downs. Many of these standing stones were felled in the Middle Ages, and others were broken up using fire and water in the seventeenth and eighteenth centuries. Where the sites of these were located in the 1930s by the owner and excavator, the marmalade-maker millionaire Alexander Keiller, the stones have been re-erected or their sites marked by concrete posts. This can all be seen clearly in the western (right-hand) side of figure 40. To the south (top of the picture) is an avenue of pairs of stones, the Kennet Avenue, again with many of them restored or re-erected. This avenue of pairs of stones runs south-eastwards for almost three kilometres to a monument called, by the early antiquaries, the Sanctuary. This site which originally consisted of a series of stone and wooden circles was broken up also in the eighteenth century (41). As can be seen, the stone and post positions are now marked by concrete posts. It formed the end of the avenue linked to the main circle at Avebury and must have been an important element in the whole scheme. We now know, as a result of recent research, that there was another avenue coming out of the west entrance of the henge (down the village street) and

38, 39 Knap Hill causewayed enclosure – the lines are later trackways and in the centre is the Romano-British farmstead

40 (Above left) *Avebury from the north-west*

41 (Above) *The Sanctuary (centre) with Bronze Age round barrows above*

42 (Left) *Avebury from the east with the earthworks of the henge and the medieval village*

running at least two kilometres to the west. This Beckhampton Avenue had been recorded by the antiquary William Stukeley in the eighteenth century. It seems at least possible that there might be avenues leaving the north and east entrances of the henge as well and that these wait to be discovered in the future.

Inside Avebury are the remains of two further stone circles themselves bigger than almost any other stone circles elsewhere in Britain. Parts of these have been restored but much still lies buried. The eastern half of Avebury has not been excavated and was not restored in the 1930s (42). In this part can be seen the un-restored earthworks of the henge together with the later features of the medieval village which elsewhere have been removed. The village boundary bank and the croft boundaries of the eastern end of the medieval village can still be seen here as well as several platforms marking the sites of abandoned medieval houses. The main road from London to Bath formerly ran through the site and the wide lane of this can be seen together with houses that have encroached upon it. Avebury is as good a medieval and post-medieval village site as it is a prehistoric one!

Just outside Avebury, but again forming part of the complex, is Silbury Hill, the largest artificial prehistoric mound in Europe and built in stages from 2750 BC (43). The quarry ditches dug to acquire the chalk to build it can still be seen, especially when they are flooded. The drums of chalk, making it look like a giant wedding cake, can only be appreciated towards the top and in certain light (44). Recent research suggests that originally there might have been a spiral path winding up the mound.

While a number of these pictures show examples of Bronze Age round barrows, there must formerly have been many more. This landscape, unlike that around Stonehenge, has been affected considerably by the activities of later farmers. For example, just to the south of the henge on Waden Hill (45) there can be seen the soil marks of ploughed out barrows – perhaps at least 7 of them – which formerly existed as mounds visible on top of the hill.

The Avebury region continued to be intensively used in the post-Roman period. Figure 46 shows the Wansdyke, a huge Saxon boundary earthwork, which runs from near Bath in the west to Savernake Forest in east Wiltshire. The

43, 44 Silbury Hill – the mound with the flooded quarry ditches

45 Waden Hill, south of Avebury, with the soil marks of former barrows

exact date of its construction is not known though it is assumed to be some time in the sixth to ninth centuries. Also its purpose is unclear. The ditch is on the north side so logically it could have been built by the Wessex kings in the south against anticipated expansion by the kingdom of Mercia to the north. Equally it could have defended Britons to the south from incoming Saxons.

Further reading

Aubrey Burl, *Prehistoric Avebury*, Yale 1979

Caroline Malone, *Avebury*, Batsford English Heritage 1989

Stuart Piggott, *The West Kennet Long Barrow Excavations 1955-56*, London HMSO 1962

Joshua Pollard & Andrew Reynolds, *Avebury: Biography of a Landscape,* Tempus 2002

Peter Ucko *et al.*, *Avebury Reconsidered: From the 1660s to the 1990s,* London Unwin Hyman 1991

46 Wansdyke, from the west, running across the downland south of Avebury; to the left are hollows of numerous road lines

4

GEAR & THE HELFORD RIVER, CORNWALL

Cornwall typically has a landscape of irregularly shaped and sized fields with narrow deep winding lanes running between a scattered pattern of farmsteads. Figure 47 shows the south Cornwall landscape near the Helford River, not far from the Lizard. This is what we see here with the addition of steep wooded slopes along the edges of the Helford river itself.

The Helford river is one of a large number of drowned river valleys or 'rias' along the coast of south-west England (48); others can be seen at Falmouth and Plymouth. These tidal waters now prove a real obstacle to vehicular traffic so that the places where bridges could be easily built became important communication centres; elsewhere in earlier times ferries crossing these rias were very important. There are a number of famous ferries in

Cornwall, such as King Harry Ferry near Truro on the River Fal. Towards the sea on this picture there was another at Helford Passage (the old local name for a ferry) providing access for Helford village to the north side of the river. It was of course much easier to move around areas like this by boat using the coast and the miles of tidal water inland. There are large numbers of quays and jetties including Bishop's Quay which is more or less under the helicopter in this shot. When the tide goes out these rias have mudflats and sand banks rich in seashore food resources.

Cornwall is an area with a lot of early settlement dating back to the prehistoric period (49). In that aspect it is not exceptional as we can now see that much of the British

47 *Gear (left centre) and the Helford river (right) from the east*

landscape was intensively used over the last three to four millennia. But much of this is still visible in Cornwall where prehistoric burial chambers, stone circles and settlement sites still survive intact, whereas elsewhere they have been ploughed out by later agricultural activity. In the centre of this picture can be seen one of the largest prehistoric enclosures in Cornwall surviving as a great tree-covered bank with a ditch on the outside. Extensive geophysical survey of the whole of the interior, together with a field survey of the ploughed (brown) segment and selective excavation, has shown that the whole of the interior was occupied by round Iron Age houses with their paddocks, enclosures and trackways. If all of this was occupied at the same time then this would have been a densely occupied settlement of probably several hundred people. Its Cornish name is 'Gear', derived from 'caer' meaning an enclosure or fortification.

Such sites would not have existed in isolation. One of the great achievements of landscape archaeology over the last 30 years is to provide some of the evidence of the contemporary surroundings of such sites. We know that a trackway left the enclosure from the main gate and ran down to the river, off to the right where presumably there was a 'port' or landing place of some sort. It is also likely that at least part of the pattern of fields dates back to the late prehistoric period, as has been observed elsewhere in Cornwall. Once the massive earth and stone field banks of these fields had been laid down it would be a mammoth task, perhaps impossible, to redesign the whole landscape layout again. We can expect modification in succeeding centuries but not for the slate to be completely wiped clean with each farming generation.

There would also have been other settlements in the landscape around such a large enclosure. These might have been occupied by local chiefs each on their own estate, or by the 'tenant' farmers who worked the land for the wealthier sections of society. Many places survive in

48 *The Helford river looking towards the coast*

ological features which would have affected crop growth, have disappeared. Mapping these sites from surviving earthworks and cropmark sites suggests that the landscape was densely scattered with such farm sites, rather like it still is with the current pattern of scattered isolated farms. There is therefore no reason why many of the sites of the presently occupied farms, and the fields that they work, should not be at least 2,000 years old in a landscape like this.

Further reading

Susan Pearce, *The Archaeology of South West Britain,* Collins London 1981

Malcolm Todd, *The South West to AD 1000,* Longman Harlow 1987

49 (Above) *The enclosure at Gear with the bank and ditch topped with trees*

50 (Right) *Cropmark of a circular enclosure probably indicating a prehistoric farm site*

Cornwall which probably represent these sites, either as collections of round houses in enclosures, as the earthworks of the usually circular enclosures themselves, or as the place names of existing farms incorporating 'caer'. Even in Cornwall, which is a relatively well-researched county and where so much survives as upstanding monuments, new discoveries can still be made. Figure **50** shows the cropmark of a circular enclosure on a flat promontory projecting into the valley of the Helford river. The deeper, wetter soil in the ditches is keeping the crop green while all around it is ripening and turning yellow. The right-hand side has no trace of the rest of the circle as here the crop is already ripe and any effects of the differences in available soil moisture, caused by buried archae-

5

HADRIAN'S WALL, BIRDOSWALD FORT & BEWCASTLE

Hadrian's Wall is probably the most famous Roman monument in Britain. At Birdoswald Roman fort in Cumbria there is a microcosm of the development of the whole defensive system of the Wall (**51**). The fort itself (probably called Banna by the Romans) is of the usual playing-card shape of Roman forts (**52**) with rounded corners with towers and gates in each of the sides (**53**) and towers along the walls. Inside were barrack blocks, granaries, a headquarters building and numerous other structures most of which still lie buried and unexcavated at the site (**54**). The fort began as a timber structure with turf-built defences. It was rebuilt in stone and eventually was accompanied by a very extensive civil settlement – or vicus – stretching out to east and west along the plateau top along the road on either side of the fort (**55**). Nothing can be seen of this now, though it is clear on geophysical surveys, and it has been examined in limited excavations as has the adjacent cemetery.

Figure **55** shows the dramatic siting of the fort. To the north are extensive bogs and marshes while to the south is

51 *Birdoswald Roman fort from the south with the River Irthing in the foreground*

the steep escarpment overlooking the River Irthing. The river here has eroded the escarpment considerably over the last almost two millennia removing much of the land south of the fort including much of the first phase of defences in this part of the Wall. Excavations in this area have shown from preserved pollen deposits that the countryside was wooded with peat bogs when the Roman army came to this area.

Recent excavations in the fort have exposed the massive stone-built granaries used to store the cereals on which the garrison depended (**56**), and the elaborate west gate of the fort. At the end of the Roman period in the fifth century the northern granary was turned into the base of a great timber hall, probably the headquarters of a local post-Roman chieftain and now marked out with timber posts. The same thing seems to have happened at other forts elsewhere on the Wall.

Near Birdoswald most of the features associated with the development of the Wall can still be seen. Half a kilometre to the east of the fort is a well-preserved milecastle at Harrow's Scar (**57**). As the name suggests these were built

52 (Above) *Birdoswald Roman fort from the north*

53 (Left) *The east gate of the fort with a square tower on each side*

54 (Below) *Birdoswald Roman fort*

55 (Right) *The location of the fort on a plateau above the River Irthing to the south. The civil settlement (or 'vicus') spreads out either side of the fort*

56 (Below right) *The excavated granaries of the Roman fort with the tower house and farm nearby*

Opposite

57 (Above left) *Harrow's Scar milecastle from the north*

58 (Below left) *Harrow's Scar milecastle above the River Irthing from the east, with the Wall and former bridge site of Willowford in the foreground*

59 (Right) *Willowford from the north-east – the line of the Wall where it crossed the River Irthing by a bridge with a mill*

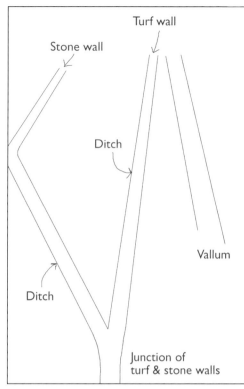

every Roman mile along the wall and each had a couple of barrack blocks built inside for the detachment of troops. This one over-looked the escarpment down to the River Irthing to the east (**58**). Here at Willowford was one of the places the Wall crossed a river (the others were at Carlisle across the River Eden and at Chesters where the River North Tyne was crossed). The river has moved further west towards the escarpment since Roman times leaving the bridge and a probable Roman water mill stranded on the flood plain. A well-preserved section of the wall links the bridge to a turret on the higher land (**59**).

Before the stone wall was built to the west of Birdoswald there was a turf rampart accompanied by a ditch on the north side. This was replaced by the stone wall on the same course for most of its length except for a small section of two to three kilometres west of Birdoswald fort where the later stone wall followed a line somewhat north of the turf wall. The whole defensive system was eventually backed on the south side by a system of ditch and banks – the vallum – which in effect defined the military zone of the Wall. Figure **60** shows the line of the turf wall with its ditch, the line of the Wall, though it is robbed out and replaced by a road, its frontal ditch, and the line of the vallum. These are still prominent earthworks (**61**) in the farmland amid the enclosed fields and shelter belts of the post-medieval landscape.

60 and **plan** *The turf wall and vallum west of Birdoswald*

61 *The line of the turf wall across the centre, with the line of the vallum above surviving as earthworks in the farmland*

Bewcastle (**62**) lies some ten kilometres away from Birdoswald, to which it was linked by a Roman road, in the wild country to the north of Hadrian's Wall. There are many contrasts with Birdoswald and yet the Roman fort here was occupied at the same time and it was part of the same elaborate defensive frontier system. There were few other forts in front of the wall, in 'enemy' territory, so there may be additional reasons other than military considerations for the use of Bewcastle. As with Hadrian's Wall generally this was not unoccupied territory before and during the Roman occupation – otherwise why would the Roman army be here – and there were native settlements all over the place. At Bewcastle there may also have been a native shrine that was taken over by the Romans. The Roman name for the site was *Fanum Cocidii* – Temple of Cocidius – and an altar and two silver plaques dedicated to this god have been found in the fort. The site of the shrine is not known – it could have been on the plateau top occupied by the fort – but there is still a spring to the north-west which may have been the focus (**62**).

62 (Above left) *Bewcastle from the east*

63 (Left) *Bewcastle with the castle and its wide ditches in the foreground*

64 (Above) *Bewcastle – the castle and the farm*

65 *Bewcastle from the north with the Roman road heading southwards*

The fort itself is a great contrast to Birdoswald because it is very irregular in shape, the line of the defences following the outline of the hill (**62**). The interior is now occupied by a Norman castle, in the north-east corner of the fort, together with a farm and the parish church (**63**). The castle sits on a wide rectangular platform with a wide ditch, the construction of which destroyed much of the interior of the fort (**64**). The church and its graveyard occupy much of the southern half of the plateau and the digging of the graves over the centuries must have disturbed the Roman archaeology a good deal. Next to the church, but not

visible on these air photographs, is the very large and fine shaft of a decorated cross of the seventh or eighth century incorporating a sundial. The most likely context for such a monument is an early monastery and so it is possible that the Roman fort enclosure was reused in the post-Roman centuries as a religious enclosure. Excavations in the open area between the castle and the church have located the main buildings of the Roman fort.

The view from the north (**65**) shows the road heading off south to Birdoswald (and civilization?) while all around is

Opposite

66 (Above) *The border landscape near Bewcastle*

67 (Below left) *The uplands were used for summer pasture – note the pound and the sheilings*

68 (Below right) *A ruined sheiling – a house used for summer visits when pasturing animals*

relatively empty countryside even today (**66**). This whole Hadrian's Wall region was for a long time border territory, disputed and fought over by rival families and clans. There are many castles and later fortified houses built in a response to this. The best-known period for this raiding was the sixteenth and seventeenth centuries when the so-called border reivers – family gangs of cattle thieves and rustlers engaged in inter-clan feuds – made the whole area unsafe to live in and travel through. Cattle and sheep formed the mainstay of the economy, and also the main reason for much of the raiding. On the bleak uplands there was little activity in the winter but in spring and summer they were occupied temporarily by shepherds. The sheilings they lived in and the enclosures for corralling the animals remain dotted all over the uplands (**67, 68**). There are very many castles, fortified houses and towers in this region as families only felt safe from raiding living in a fortified house. One of the finest, a little further to the north, is Hermitage Castle. There probably was a hermitage here originally in this bleak part of the Scottish southern uplands, though the castle controlled the route along Liddesdale from England into Scotland (**69**). The castle dates from the thirteenth century but the present structure is fourteenth century when a tower house was added to the earlier rectangular enclosure (**70**). Earthworks around indicate further enclosures, wet moats and fishponds.

The area of southern Scotland and northern England is in many ways a good example of a landscape of conflict rather like the Welsh border counties or Flanders in north-west Europe. Peace finally came to this whole border region in the seventeenth century, when the crowns of

69, 70 *Hermitage Castle – the stone buildings and the earthworks of enclosures, moats and fishponds*

England and Scotland were combined, after nearly two thousand years of military activity of one sort or another, including the Roman occupation and the building of Hadrian's Wall. Settlement and agriculture were developed in the eighteenth and nineteenth centuries with investment in estates and communications. Newcastleton (**71**) encapsulates these later peaceful aspects of the border. It was founded in 1793 by the third Duke of Buccleuch as an estate village to house hand-loom weavers. It is based on a grid plan of streets and lanes with three open squares spaced evenly along the main road. It harks back to the planned towns of the Middle Ages in England and forward to the grid plans of innumerable new towns founded by north Europeans in other parts of the world.

Further reading

Guy de la Bédoyère, *Hadrian's Wall: History and Guide*, Tempus Stroud 1998

David Breeze & Brian Dobson, *Hadrian's Wall*, Penguin 1987

G.D.B. Jones & D.J. Wooliscroft, *Hadrian's Wall from the air*, Tempus Stroud 2001

Stephen Johnson, *Hadrian's Wall*, Batsford/English Heritage 1989

Godfrey Watson, *The Border Reivers*, Robert Hale 1974

Tony Wilmott, *Birdoswald Roman Fort: 1800 Years on Hadrian's Wall*, Tempus Stroud 2001

71 *Newcastleton planned village*

6

ROMAN SITES IN THE COTSWOLDS

The Cotswolds in Gloucestershire have one of the densest areas of Roman villas in the country, matched only by the hinterlands of Bath and Ilchester in Somerset and parts of the south-east and the Home Counties. The Fosse Way links the first two areas which all had access to fine building stone for the construction of elaborate villa buildings. In the Cotswolds there was also the important Roman urban centre at Cirencester, the cantonal capital of the Dobunni tribe – *Corinium Dobunnorum* – and major religious complexes such as Bath (the Roman *Aquae Sulis*).

There is little evidence of military activity in this area from the first phases of the Roman conquest, although it is assumed that there were forts in the area, even if only for a short period, and it is known there was a fort under Cirencester. The nearest legionary base was at Gloucester. It has been suggested that the Fosse Way (**72**) was built some time in the AD 40s as a frontier road behind (that is to the east of) the actual Roman frontier with the British to the west. It cuts directly across country on the high ground of the Cotswolds and would have been ideal if there were forts to the west of it.

72 *The Fosse Way looking north at Fossebridge where it crosses the River Coln*

Later it formed one of the major highways of Roman Britain linking up some of the most important towns.

At Cirencester there is little to be seen from the Roman period, and except for the outline of the town walls the earlier topography seems to have had little influence on later developments. One rare survival however is the great amphitheatre just outside the town's defences (**73**). This has the usual two opposing entrances together with great banks that would have supported the seating. Bath has little of the Roman town (**74**) left to see beyond the splendid baths themselves. It is now generally assumed that the course of the Roman town wall, which influenced the layout of the later town, may have only enclosed the spring, baths and temple complex, and that any urban population was outside this, probably to the north at Walcot. The baths and temple temenos (temple enclosure) complex (**75**) occupy the centre of the walled area, still in the centre of the town. They were refurbished again and again, in the Middle Ages under Bishop John de Villula, and later as part of the spa complex created at Bath in the eighteenth century. Today the magnificent, prolific hot

73 *The ampitheatre at Cirencester, Gloucestershire*

75 *Bath – the central area with the abbey church, the Roman baths and the eighteenth-century pump room*

74 and **plan** *Bath – the central area of the town with the line of the Roman and medieval town wall*

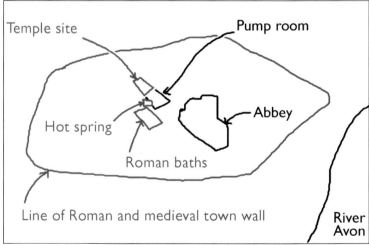

spring and the adjacent large Roman swimming pool (76) form part of the complex of eighteenth-century spa buildings including the Pump Room, while the bathing establishments themselves, though still accessible, are largely underground beneath later buildings.

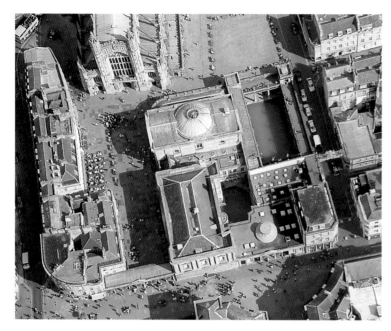

76 and **plan** *Bath – the Roman baths, with the hot spring next to the pump room*

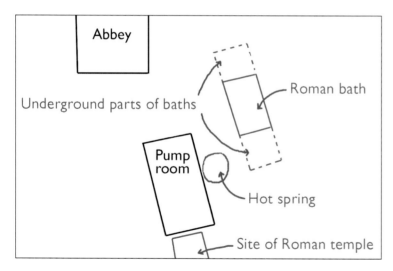

All around these centres were the villa estates surrounding the large country houses that developed through the Roman centuries. The most famous and accessible of these in this region is at Chedworth, where the villa was discovered in 1864 and given to the National

Trust in 1924. It is beautifully situated at the top end of a short east-facing valley overlooking the River Coln. Here a large spring pours out; this was used as a water supply, to supply the baths and as the focus for a water cult with a small temple (**77**). The ranges of buildings were laid out around the valley head, to the north, south and west. The sequence of construction of these has been worked out from recent excavations, together with the development of the two bathhouses, one for damp heat (Turkish) and one for dry (sauna). There are also fine elaborate mosaics and impressive hypocaust heating systems on the site. The modern roofing of these to protect the ruins, together with the construction of the custodian's house to the east of the main buildings (**78**), can confuse the visitor, or the

77 *The Chedworth Roman villa from the east*

53

78 *Chedworth Roman villa – the house is nineteenth-century and some of the Roman buildings have modern covers*

79, 80 *Turkdean, Gloucestershire – the cropmarks of the large Roman villa*

viewer from the air, into thinking that these are all Roman structures.

Perhaps surprisingly, such Roman villa complexes still turn up on a regular basis. Hardly a year goes by without another example being discovered even in well-researched areas like the Cotswolds. Most of these are out in the open countryside, suggesting a complete change in settlement pattern between the Roman period and the Middle Ages. However others are known to exist under or next to later villages where there might be an argument for some sort of continuity of estate or agricultural land-use from one period to another.

At Turkdean in a very remote part of the Cotswolds a large villa was found by the observation of parchmarks in the grass from the air. In 1997 when excavations were carried out, the lines of parched out grass over the buried walls could be clearly seen at ground level, let alone from

81 *The site of the Turkdean villa (mid-left) on a bench on the valley side*

82 *Turkdean Roman villa from the north with springs to the south (top)*

the air (**79**). The detail is extraordinary with evidence of ranges of buildings, corridors, boundary walls and garden areas showing up clearly (**80**). All of this indicates a very large villa with buildings arranged around two adjacent courtyards. The villa sits on a bench on the valley side, looking west (**81**). There are numerous springs to the south (**82**) but the main spring, which probably supplied the villa with water and where there may have been a temple, is up the slope to the north-east. It still produces a prodigious quantity of water daily.

Not all of the settlement in the Cotswolds was either towns or villas in the Roman period. There must have been large numbers of ordinary farmsteads, which have left very little trace and which will probably only ever show up as cropmarks on aerial photographs. There must also have been many villages or small market towns, similar in size and function to those found on the Cotswolds in the

83 (Left) *Whitcomb looking towards Andoversford*

84 and **plan** (Above and opposite) *Whitcomb*

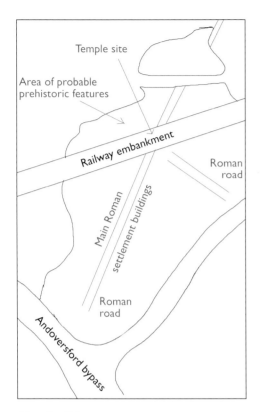

Plan for **84**

85 *Whitcomb cropmarks of probable prehistoric features including ring ditches of houses or long barrows*

Middle Ages. Again it is only from aerial photography or systematic fieldwork that these are likely to be recognized. A good example is the site (we do not know its Roman name) at Whitcomb near Andoversford. This site has been known for some time and was crossed by a railway in the nineteenth century – the embankment for this across the site is still the most prominent feature in the fields. In June 2000 the settlement was showing up particularly well as cropmarks in a growing cereal crop, despite the wet weather in previous weeks. The settlement of enclosures and buildings lies along a branch road between the Ermin Way and the Fosse Way and this appears as a light line in the crop (**83**). The alignment of this road as a cropmark makes it clear that the local lanes to the south-west (**83**) and north-east (**84**) also date in origin at least from the

Roman period. These are not the straight direct highways we usually associate with the major Roman roads and they therefore remind us that many of the lanes and tracks in our present landscape can have their origins in the Roman period at least, if not before.

There was certainly prehistoric activity in the vicinity of the Roman site as finds have been made in the nearby gravel pit. Indeed some of the cropmarks look as if they are caused by prehistoric features, such as either the ring ditches of former barrows or of later prehistoric round houses (**85**). As can be seen, these are very close to the road with its buildings (**86**). Although a temple is known at the site, roughly under the railway embankment, the main characteristic of the settlement, which is typical of these small towns/villages, is that each side of the road is

57

86 *Whitcomb showing Roman road and building foundations; the darker circles may be prehistoric features*

lined with stone and timber buildings facing the road. These are indicated by lighter areas of crop, where they are parched out over the buried stone foundations (**87**).

In the Cotswolds in the Romano-British period, as elsewhere in the country, much of the present landscape probably dates back to the Roman period at least if not long before that. It is likely that many of the medieval and modern villages originated as Roman villas or villages and that boundaries of estates and parishes go back to that time as well. Only with extensive fieldwork and selective excavation will this be properly demonstrated. But it is the air view, especially with cropmarks, that the fullest picture can be really appreciated until this research is carried out.

Further reading

Alan McWhirr, *Roman Gloucestershire*, Sutton Stroud 1981

Royal Commission on Historical Monuments (England), *Iron Age and Romano-British Monuments in the Gloucestershire Cotswolds*, London HMSO 1976

87 *Whitcomb – cropmarks of the road and the probable stone buildings of the Roman settlement on each side of it*

7

BRADING & THE ISLE OF WIGHT

The Brading area of the Isle of Wight illustrates how a landscape can be dramatically altered by natural processes over a long period. Figure **88** shows a large part of the southeastern part of the Isle of Wight. In the foreground is the site of the impressive Roman villa at Brading (**89**). Some of the buildings have their foundations marked out (right, in white) while the main Roman buildings with the best-preserved mosaics are under the large shed (some idea of the size can be gained from the coach parked in the car park). The villa sits in the middle of fertile arable land with pasture and woodland beyond. On the hill at the back overlooking the sea is a large Victorian fort – Bembridge Fort (**92**).

However, this modern view is deceptive and does not represent the proper context for the villa in its heyday. Across the centre of the picture, all the flat land that can be seen was formerly a sea channel between the sea at the top of the picture and the present south coast of the Isle of Wight off to the right. With this reconstructed in the mind's eye we can see that the land beyond would in fact

88 *Brading with the Roman villa in the south-east of the Isle of Wight*

have been an island off the Isle of Wight in Roman times. A further Roman site, though not a villa, has been excavated here. It may have been related to the villa at Brading as the narrowest and shallowest part of the sea channel is crossed by a causeway of unknown date linking the two islands.

Figure **90** clearly shows this former sea channel between the two areas of 'higher' ground which would have been flood free. It can be seen that the flat land is crossed with streams, former river meanders and early drainage ditch features. So when the sea no longer came this far inland the area clearly had a number of streams and small rivers flowing across it. As these lowland areas were reclaimed and dried out so that they could be used for pasture farming, water would be removed in the drainage ditches. Many areas around the coast of Britain are like this.

The village of Brading (**91**) begins to make sense once we realise that it was formerly adjacent to open navigable water. From the air it looks like a typical village with the church at one end of the street. However the properties

89 The Roman villa site at Brading

90 The former sea channel, now reclaimed, with marshes, meanders and streams

are very densely packed as in medieval towns. There is also a small former town hall near the church. It was indeed formerly a borough, from at least 1547, but significantly it was also a port with ships landing to the east just off the top of the picture.

The Victorian fort (92) serves to remind us that at all periods the Isle of Wight was heavily fortified in case of seaborne invasion. There is a possible 'Saxon Shore' type of fort of the late Roman period in the middle of the island at Carisbrooke, where there is also a large medieval castle. Several other settlements were equipped with forts and defences in the Middle Ages. However it was in the nineteenth century that most was invested in defences for the island. Near to the Isle of Wight was the great naval base of Portsmouth and anchorage for the fleet at Spithead. This was heavily defended with outer forts including those on the Isle of Wight. The fear of invasion from the French under Napoleon III in the middle of the nineteenth century led to many self-contained gun batteries being built around its coast – the so-called Palmerston's follies. Often these were of brick with extensive earthen ramparts. Huge cast-iron guns were housed in armoured casements with extensive magazines for gunpowder and shells nearby and accommodation for the soldiers. While now redundant, often overgrown and frequently in inappropriate use, they are still very impressive features in the landscape.

The completely silted up former area of the sea reminds us, however, that at any time in the past the landscape could have looked considerably different to the way it does today. This is particularly true of low-lying areas round the coast which were formerly flooded and which have been subsequently drained and reclaimed. In order to see the context for the earlier sites, and for a full appreciation of subsequent changes to be possible, some attempt needs to be made to reconstruct the earlier landscape that was contemporary with any site that is under investigation.

91 (Above) *Brading village – the former medieval town and port*

92 (Right) *The nineteenth-century Bembridge fort*

Further reading

Andrew Saunders, *Fortress Britain – Artillery Fortification in the British Isles and Ireland*, Beaufort, Liphook Hants 1989

8

HOLY ISLAND & HARTLEPOOL

Holy Island or Lindisfarne is one of the most important early Christian sites in the British Isles. A monastery was founded in 635 by St Aidan, who had been sent from the Irish monastery of Iona in Scotland to convert the people of Northumbria at the invitation of Oswald, the Anglo-Saxon king of Bernicia. Aidan seems to have chosen a site very typical for an 'Irish' type of monastery – an island off the coast only accessible at low tide (94). (Iona, off the west coast of the island of Mull in Scotland, is similarly situated.) Here a monastery was built not only to act as a cathedral and missionary centre for the Northumbrians, specifically the Bernicians in north Northumbria, but also a place of peace and contemplation for the monks. It was near to the royal centres at Yeavering inland and Bamburgh on the coast. The buildings of the monastery, almost certainly of wood at that time, have not survived though the ruined medieval priory buildings, which can be seen today, are probably on the same site (93), a flat area in the south-west corner of the island. These consist of a roofless monastic church and adjacent

93 *The ruins of the medieval priory at Lindisfarne with St Cuthbert's Church (bottom left)*

cloister surrounded by the domestic buildings. To the west is the surviving medieval parish church of St Cuthbert (96). This and the priory church may be on the sites of several Anglo-Saxon monastic churches as they are in line with each other. This seems to have been a common arrangement at this time with monasteries having several churches aligned in a row. Other enclosures around these buildings housed the offices for the monastery such as the barns, bakery, brew-house, stables and guest accommodation.

It is difficult for us now to imagine the immense importance of this seventh-century monastery. It became a great centre of learning and teaching. In particular it became famous as a centre of scholarship and book production. A series of volumes are known that were produced here including the world famous 'Lindisfarne Gospels' and the Codex Amiatinus, highly decorated illuminated manuscripts. These required large numbers of sheep skins for the pages, and rare and expensive pigments and gold leaf for the illustrations.

94 *The causeway exposed at low tide linking the mainland with Lindisfarne*

95 *St Cuthbert's Island off Lindisfarne with the medieval priory in the background*

96 *The medieval priory with St Cuthbert's Church and the Heugh in the background*

97 *St Cuthbert's Island with the site of a chapel and foundations visible*

The monastery lasted for nearly two hundred years as a great centre until it was destroyed by the Danes. Its most famous monk was Cuthbert who died in 687 and is now buried in Durham Cathedral. The monastery was refounded in the late eleventh century as a cell of Durham cathedral priory.

The buildings were situated in a precinct on a flat area at the south-west corner of the main island (**95**). This is not now defined by a visible wall or bank but its outline is reflected in the layout of the streets. The site of the priory, and the earlier monastery, were sheltered from the south behind a ridge of volcanic rock called the Heugh, while much of the present village also occupies areas of the former monastic enclosure. Parts of the early monastery have recently been excavated in the middle of the village.

Such monasteries in the Anglo-Saxon period often had subsidiary hermitages around them to which the monks could retreat for contemplation or at times of fasting like Lent. We know that Cuthbert spent much time in his hermitage on the islet of Inner Farne in the Farne islands just off the coast near Bamburgh. There is also a small island, St Cuthbert's Island, with a chapel and other building foundations just off the south-west corner of Lindisfarne itself which must have been another hermitage site (**97**).

The position of the monastery right next to the sea made it vulnerable to coastal raiders especially as it was largely undefended. Indeed the monastery was one of the first casualties of Viking attacks when it was burnt down and many monks killed in 793.

Coastal defence has remained a persistent landscape feature in such situations. A medieval castle was built on Lindisfarne in the Middle Ages though it was refurbished and extensively altered by Edwin Lutyens in the twentieth century (**98**). In the sixteenth century a sheltered harbour here was used as a victualling (or supply) base for the navy with a defended yard within the area of the former priory (**99**). As at Brading the coast has subsequently altered with much of the former harbour becoming silted up and now being dry land, although it can still be seen in the low-lying land and the small cliff-line formerly marking the back of the beach.

Hartlepool, though very different in appearance today, has an amazingly similar landscape history in the Anglo-Saxon period. The dramatic peninsula (**100**) may well have been an island just off the coast in earlier times. Not only is it now connected to the mainland by a narrow isthmus (which seems to be mainly peat deposits) but the coastline has been altered with the construction of docks and the partial infilling of the sheltered lagoon behind the peninsula. Because the town is now dominated by rows of terraced nineteenth- and twentieth-century housing it is difficult to appreciate that there was a medieval walled town with a port here 800 years ago. One of the town gates survives (**101**) and the high street of the medieval town is now incongruously a road in a housing estate.

98 *Lindisfarne Castle*

99 *The harbour and silted-up area at Lindisfarne*

100 *Hartlepool on its peninsula with the North Sea to the east (right)*

101 *The site of the medieval town and port of Hartlepool with the remaining town gate in the surviving town wall*

Perhaps the greatest surprise within such an urban landscape is the existence of one of the most important Anglo-Saxon nunneries in England. The present parish church of St Hilda (**102**), which dates only from the Middle Ages, is nevertheless in the middle of what was the former monastery. This was excavated as old housing and other buildings were cleared and the areas laid out as public open space. Some of these have been excavated

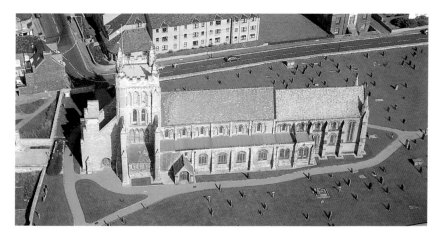

102 *Hartlepool – the medieval church of St Hilda*

and we now know quite a lot about the timber buildings, industrial activity and cemetery areas of the monastery.

Hartlepool was founded in about 640 by Heiu just after Lindisfarne. It was given by Aidan to Hild who organised it as an Anglo-Saxon double monastery of monks and nuns under her supervision as abbess. She moved to Whitby to found a similar monastery there in 657, and from then we hear no more about Hartlepool. Finds of grave slabs however indicate the site on the headland. The sites of Lindisfarne and Hartlepool monasteries are so similar that it is almost as if the founders of the nunnery picked a site which was topographically almost identical to the earlier and revered site at Lindisfarne some way north further up the coast.

From these sites and others like them missionaries set out to convert Anglo-Saxon England to Christianity before Augustine and his followers were able to convert the Saxon kingdoms in the south. Their influence was especially felt in Northumbria (roughly from Northumberland south to Lincolnshire) and Mercia (the Midland counties). Considerable progress had been made before the Synod of Whitby in 664, after which 'Roman' missionaries rather than Irish had a greater influence in the development of the English Church.

Further reading

Gerald Bonner, David Rollason & Clare Stancliffe (eds), *St Cuthbert, his Cult and his Community to AD 1200*, Boydell Woodbridge 1989

Jane Hawkes & Susan Mills (eds), *Northumbria's Golden Age*, Sutton Stroud 1999

Robin Daniels, 'The Anglo-Saxon Monastery at Hartlepool, England' in *Northumbria's Golden Age* edited by Jane Hawkes & Susan Mills, Sutton Stroud 1999

N.J. Higham, *The Kingdom of Northumbria AD 350-1100*, Alan Sutton Stroud 1993

Deirdre O'Sullivan & Robert Young, *Lindisfarne Holy Island*, Batsford/English Heritage 1995

9

ATHELNEY, SOMERSET

Athelney, and the landscape around it, is one of the most important sites of Anglo-Saxon England. It was here in the marshes of central Somerset in 878 that Alfred regrouped and reorganised his army before going on to defeat the Danish king Guthrum and his Scandinavian army at the battle of Edington (Wiltshire). If this had not happened England may well have become part of a long-lived kingdom based on Denmark or Norway.

Why did Alfred choose Athelney as his base? Looked at

103 *Athelney Island (top left) with the causeway to Lyng (bottom right)*

1374-5 the river was diverted and the island linked to the mainland by a causeway – the Balt Moor Wall. All around the low-lying land flooded regularly, the marshes and swamps providing natural defences for the island. Asser, Alfred's biographer, tells us Athelney was 'surrounded on all sides by very swampy and impassable marshes so that no one can approach it by any means except punts'. William of Malmesbury writing in the twelfth century says 'Athelney is not an island of the sea, but

on the regional scale Athelney was hidden away in the Somerset marshes some long way away from the centres of fighting and the bases of the Danish army which were much further to the east, at Chippenham and Reading for example. So Athelney was well back from the front line.

Looked at in its local landscape, however, Athelney was an ideal spot. It is in effect an inland 'island' – the name means 'isle of the princes' – off the end of an eastern projecting peninsula, on which the village of Lyng is built (102). Indeed it was separated from the 'mainland' by a branch of the former course of the River Tone. Later in

it is so inaccessible on account of bogs and the inundation of the lakes, that it cannot be got to but in a boat . . . the firm land, which is only two acres in breadth'.

The River Parrett is also to the east, no doubt acting as a barrier to any approach from that direction. Within the wide marshy floodable valley of the Parrett, the only easy crossing place was at the narrow point of the valley at Langport (104). Here was constructed a fort, on the eastern side of the river, which was later recorded in the tenth-century document, the Burghal Hidage. While there may have been a fort to the west of the crossing of the

104 *Langport from the east with the River Parrett. In the foreground was the Anglo-Saxon fort*

105 *Burrow Mump and the River Parrett*

Parrett as well, on Hurd's Hill, it is significant that the main fort was to the east, in effect a bridgehead defence for the river crossing and a barrier to anyone approaching from the east. Alfred's base at Athelney was part of a rather wider scheme of the defence of central Somerset. It probably included Burrow Mump, near to Athelney, and perhaps significantly on the eastern side of the Parrett. This large prominent natural mound was too small for a fort, but it would have been ideal as a landmark for people approaching Athelney and as a signalling point (**105**). On top is a later castle and chapel.

Recent excavations (2002) have shown that there was an Iron Age ditch and rampart around the western end of Athelney and this may be why Alfred chose the site. Perhaps Alfred knew of these old defences on this low-lying site which could, with very little effort, be refurbished with a new palisade of timber and a fortified gateway. Nothing of this remains on the surface today, all trace of it having been ploughed away over the centuries as the island has been used for agriculture. But the same is not true of the outer defences at the western end of Lyng village. These are the fortifications mentioned in the Burghal Hidage. David Hill has worked out, from measurements given, that these refer to a bank and ditch running from marsh to marsh and cutting off the peninsula. So that even before you reached Athelney you had to go through a gate and rampart at Lyng. This in fact is what Asser refers to in his description of the site in the late ninth century: 'a bridge has been made with laborious skill between two fortresses. At the western end of this bridge a very strong fort has been placed of most beautiful workmanship by the King's command.'

The site of the bridge can be seen on figure **106**. In the foreground the church of St Bartholomew at Lyng stands on the line of the rampart to the south of the presumed site of the gate. It is not uncommon to find early church sites over the gates of Saxon defences. The wide flattened bank and wide infilled ditch survive on the south (right-hand) side as an earthwork in the orchard. On the north

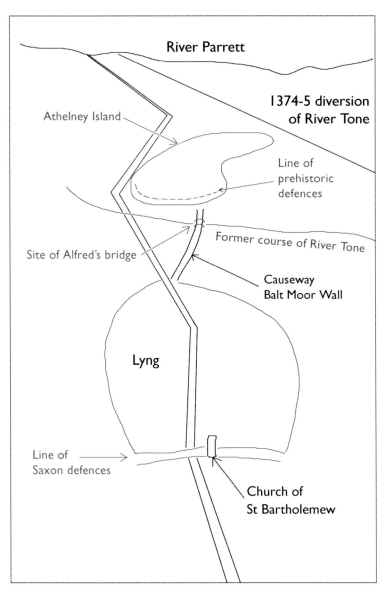

106 and **plan** *Lyng and Athelney from the west*

side its course is marked by a lane. The outline of the fort at Lyng is not as clear as it would have been in earlier times because the low-lying land around has been drained and reclaimed, but a break of slope defines the outline of the defended area. Beyond the hedge lines marking the former line of the River Tone and the later

causeway of Balt Moor Wall, Athelney (**107**) is a long sausage- or figure-of-eight-shaped area of slightly higher ground with three knolls of higher land. It is around the western one of these that the prehistoric defences have been discovered which Alfred used. All over the top of this knoll, fieldwork in 1993 and excavations in 2002 have discovered extensive evidence of iron-working, probably to be associated with the re-arming and re-equipping of Alfred's soldiers. This is very important archaeological evidence for this critical period of the history of England, and the final dating and analysis of the material from the excavations is eagerly awaited.

Alfred's campaign orchestrated from Athelney was successful. The Danish army was held in check, the Danish king, Guthrum, accepting conversion to Christianity and the new name Athelstan as part of the peace deal, and England was divided with the north-eastern counties becoming the Danelaw.

As a victory celebration and an offering of thanks, Alfred established a monastery on Athelney in 893. There was probably a hermitage already there when he took over the island since there is reference to a hermit, St Athelwine or Egelwine, and many of the islands in the Somerset marshes were inhabited at this time by hermits living an ascetic existence. It is clear that the establishment of this monastery for monks was part of a general policy by Alfred to re-establish monasticism after the disruptions of the Viking raids, and as a means of developing education which was largely carried out through the monasteries at that time. However, it proved difficult to recruit men for the monastic life. Alfred could not attract Englishmen so he recruited 'monks of various nationalities'. It is not entirely clear where either the hermitage or Alfred's monastery was sited, though it is likely that these were on the same site as the later medieval monastery, on the eastern end of the eastern knoll (**108**). A monument set

107 *The Isle of Athelney from the west with the causeway of Balt Moor Wall (bottom right)*

up in 1801 marks the site. Here geophysical survey in 1993 and excavations in 2002 clearly showed the robbed-out remains of the medieval monastic buildings together with parts of the cemetery. This Benedictine monastery was described by William of Malmesbury in the twelfth century as, 'a little monastery and dwellings for monks. Accordingly (Alfred) erected a church moderate indeed as to size but as to method of construction singular and novel: for four piers, driven into the ground, support the whole fabric, four circular chancels being drawn round it.'

This monastery and its stone successor survived for hundreds of years on the island of Athelney, surrounded by marshes which were gradually being drained and reclaimed, until it was dissolved in 1539 by Henry VIII.

Further reading

Simon Keynes & Michael Lapidge, *Alfred the Great: Asser's Life of Alfred and other contemporary sources*, Penguin 1983

William Henry Stevenson (ed.), *Asser's Life of Alfred*, Oxford Clarendon Press 1959

Michael Aston & Roger Leech, *Historic Towns of Somerset*, Bristol 1977

Michael Williams, *The Draining of the Somerset Levels*, Cambridge 1970

108 *Athelney from the north-east. The site of the monastery is to the right of the farm by the monument*

109 *Canterbury Cathedral from the west*

10

CANTERBURY, KENT

The first of the studies of historic cities looks at Canterbury in Kent. Like many of the major towns in England, Canterbury owes its origins to the choice of a site by someone in the early Roman period. Often this was a general in the army anxious to pick a good place as a base for a garrison. In other cases it was because a town was to be laid out. In the case of Canterbury it is not known if there was a fort on the site. In many cases towns were founded as administrative and market

110 Bigbury – the site of the pre-Roman hillfort on the hilltop outside Canterbury

centres for the pre-Roman tribe in the area. Bigbury, on a hill outside Canterbury (110), seems to have been the centre of the Iron Age Cantii tribe and so the development of the later city can be seen to begin with the move in the early Roman period to a more accessible lowland site by the River Stour. There a town was laid out which eventually was fully walled in the Roman period. While little remains upstanding from the Roman period, and it is largely unclear how much of the later street plan is influenced by the pattern of the underlying Roman property and road alignments, the overall shape of the

present city centre is still basically an oval. This reflects the walled Roman area straddling the River Stour, which formed the basis of the walled medieval city (111). Within this area the details of the Anglo-Saxon town also remain unclear though a lot of early Saxon houses have now been excavated. In the area of the Big Dig excavation (2001) on the east side of the city (112), new streets lined with newly-built houses seem to have been laid out in the ninth and tenth centuries. It is likely therefore that much of the present topography of Canterbury reflects an aspect of late Saxon town planning, something that we think was happening in many towns in southern England at this time.

From an earlier period it has been suggested that the area of the cathedral precinct (123), roughly the north-eastern quadrant of the Roman city defined by the lane called Burgate, was a royal enclosure for the early Kentish kings and where they probably had a palace. If this were the case it would help to explain the early importance of this area on the east side of the city (113). It became the

111 (Above left) *The oval area of the Roman and medieval city*

112 (Below) *The 'Big Dig' excavation in 2001*

113 (Above right) *The cathedral within the Burgate area of the Roman walled city with St Augustine's Abbey to the east (right)*

114 (Right) *St Augustine's Abbey with St Martin's Church (right centre)*

the site now relates to the medieval abbey (renamed St Augustine's), substantial ruins remain of the church of St Pancras as well as the foundations of the churches of St Mary and Saints Peter and Paul (**115**). These are all more or less in line, an arrangement that was a common layout of these early ecclesiastical sites (as at Holy Island). Beyond, on the site of the later cathedral, and also almost in line, were the churches of St Saviour and St John the Baptist. The monastery was the training ground for new clergy and a centre of art and learning especially under Archbishop Theodore (of Tarsus) and abbot Hadrian in the late seventh century. The cathedral was the spiritual centre for east Kent and looked after the pastoral needs of those of the local population who were Christian.

Much of what can be seen at Canterbury relates to the period after the Norman Conquest. The Dane John mound, lying on the city wall, which was originally a Roman burial mound, was modified into a motte and bailey castle (**116**), to be replaced very quickly by a

115 (Left) *St Augustine's Abbey ruins with the cathedral to the west (background) and St Pancras church ruins to the east (foreground)*

116 (Below) *The Dane John mound on the city wall*

cathedral site, as we shall see, but it was also adjacent to the earliest abbey site selected by St Augustine in his campaign to convert the English to Christianity.

The momentous events associated with this missionary activity from 597 onwards are still clear in the Canterbury landscape today. Between the city wall and the church of St Martin, which seems to have survived from Roman times and to have been used by King Aethelbert's Christian queen, Bertha, Augustine founded a monastery, dedicated to Saints Peter and Paul (a favourite early dedication) (**114**). Although much that can be seen on

117, 118 (Above left and left) *The stone Norman keep of Canterbury Castle*

119 (Above) *Canterbury town walls on the east of the city*

substantial stone-built keep (**117**, **118**). The town walls were continually maintained through the Middle Ages (**119**) and are now a major tourist attraction, as they are at York. Only one gate remains at Canterbury though, the substantial West Gate of 1380 (**120**). Much of the city was occupied with town houses, properties and gardens, and many medieval structures have survived to the present day (**121**). The main street, High Street, had many medieval lodgings built to accommodate pilgrims coming to visit the shrine of Archbishop Thomas Becket who was murdered in the cathedral in 1170.

The city then as now was dominated by the cathedral, a vast complex structure begun in its present form by Lanfranc the first Norman archbishop of Canterbury and continually modified all through the Middle Ages (**122**). There was a monastery of Benedictine monks attached to it, which later became a school, and on the west side of the precinct the archbishop's palace. The ecclesiastical enclave, the precinct with these buildings and their successors, still dominates the townscape showing up from the air as a greener open space (**123**). One of the earliest plans to have survived from the medieval period,

120 (Below) *The West Gate of 1380 at Canterbury*

121 (Right) *The West Gate and High Street with the cathedral in the background*

122 (Left) *Canterbury Cathedral*

123 (Top) *The cathedral within its medieval precinct with the former Benedictine monastery buildings on its north side (right) and the archbishop's palace beyond*

124 (Above) *The precinct of the Benedictine monastery of St Augustine's*

125 *St Augustine's Abbey – most of the buildings seen here were part of the royal palace of Henry VIII in the 1540s*

a map of 1140 showing the cathedral and its water supply, covers much of the precinct area and shows how little the arrangement of buildings has altered in the intervening centuries.

Canterbury, like any major medieval town, had a lot of monasteries. As well as the cathedral priory and St Augustine's abbey, there was St Gregory's priory, several friaries and a number of hospitals. All these were swept away at the dissolution of the monasteries under Henry VIII in the 1530s and the buildings that were not converted were demolished and their sites reused. One spectacular change occurred at St Augustine's where the abbey buildings were modified into a palace for Henry,

though he never seems to have visited it much. Behind the gatehouses of the medieval monastic precinct and among the ruins of the abbey (**124**), most of what is there on the site today relates to this post-medieval use of the site (**125**).

Further reading

Nicholas Brooks, *The Early History of the Church of Canterbury*, Leicester University Press 1984

Richard Gameson (ed.), *St Augustine and the Conversion of England*, Sutton Stroud 1999

Marjorie Lyle, *Canterbury: 2000 Years of History*, Tempus Stroud 2002

11

WINCHESTER, HAMPSHIRE

For the second of the studies of historic cities we look at Winchester in Hampshire, arguably the ancient capital of the Saxon kingdom of Wessex. Like Canterbury, Winchester owes its origins to the choice of the site, probably by a Roman general for a Roman fort. Similarly it became a tribal centre, this time for the Belgae, the Iron Age tribe of the area, and like Canterbury the lowland site replaced an earlier fortified centre. At Winchester this was at Oram's Arbour, under the west end of the town and does not seem to have affected the layout of the town. However, an earlier site is the great hillfort on St Catherine's Hill (126) which overlooks the valley of the River Itchen south of the later city.

The Roman town of *Venta Belgarum*, the administrative and market centre for the Belgae, was laid out down the slope of the west side of the valley of the Itchen. It had a grid pattern of streets and later a substantial stone town wall. Nothing of the Roman town can now be seen above the ground. Despite the grid-like plan of the streets in the northern half of the city, only the line of the Roman town

126 *The hillfort on St Catherine's Hill*

wall (127) and the positions of its gates have remained to influence the later topography. The grid plan of streets in fact belongs to the late Saxon period and may be the result of a phase of town planning associated with Alfred when he was redeveloping and refortifying a number of earlier Roman centres. This has now been recognized in a number of towns in southern England but is perhaps best represented at Winchester (128).

Characteristically, running parallel to the main street, High Street and the Broadway, there are back lanes defining the plots on the street frontage, with longer, larger plots behind. As will be seen these are rather different to the burgage plots of the properties of the new medieval towns (such as Bridgnorth and Henley in Arden).

Winchester was chosen as the seat for the bishop of the West Saxons in the seventh century following a move from Dorchester on Thames in Oxfordshire. It had several early monasteries and a nunnery. For much of its early history it was also in effect the capital of Wessex, and then England, before the ascendancy of London in the Middle Ages. As

127 *Winchester – the area of the Roman, Saxon and medieval town. The castle is on the left-hand edge*

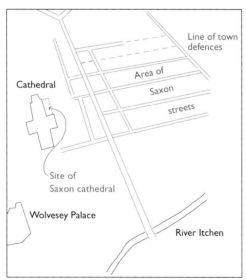

Cathedral

Line of town defences

Area of

Saxon

streets

Site of Saxon cathedral

Wolvesey Palace

River Itchen

128 and **plan** *Winchester – the layout of the Saxon streets within the Roman walled area*

such it had a royal palace and a mint to produce coins. Much of the interior of the walled area was also given over to the bishop, his residence and his cathedral.

The Normans regarded Winchester as a very important centre and somewhere that had to be taken early on in their

campaign of conquest. As in so many late Saxon towns a castle was added to the townscape, probably by taking out some of the buildings of the late Saxon city (**127**).

Figure **129** shows the south-east quadrant of the town within the Roman and medieval town walls. As at both

Canterbury and York, the ecclesiastical precinct from the Middle Ages stands out as green space in the densely built-up modern city. The present cathedral (**130**) is the building put up in the post-Norman period to replace the Anglo-Saxon cathedral, the site of which has been excavated and is now marked out in the grass. As elsewhere (Wells, Exeter)

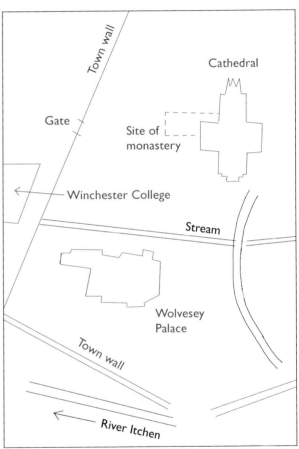

129 and **plan** *The cathedral precinct, site of the Benedictine monastery, south (left) of the cathedral and the bishop's palace at Wolvesey in the foreground*

the Normans rebuilt the cathedral on a more liturgically correct east/west alignment. This great building was not just a cathedral for the bishop, it was a Benedictine monastery as well (**130**). To the left, south of the cathedral, are the remains of the cloister and the conventual buildings of the priory of monks who occupied the site until its dissolution in 1539.

In the foreground of figure **130** are the ruins of the halls of the bishop's residence called Wolvesey Palace. This was completely walled off from the cathedral priory and was a separate set of buildings provided for the bishop, who was one of the most wealthy men in medieval England.

No doubt in the Middle Ages there were far more buildings around the palace and the cathedral, and most importantly large areas of cemeteries, but in general this would have been a much less densely developed part of the city.

Running across the lower end of the Saxon and medieval city are several streams – running from north to south – branches of the River Itchen, flowing to Southampton Water. One runs between the palace and the cathedral, another outside the walls. There were many of these streams in use in the Middle Ages for mills as well as industrial processes such as fulling and of course emptying the drains.

The influence of the medieval church at Winchester extended beyond the limits of the city walls. Immediately to the south of the Wolvesey Palace is Winchester College (**131**), founded by Bishop William of Wykeham in 1382 for poor scholars, clerics and choristers. Further away down the valley is the hospital of St Cross, founded in 1136 by Bishop Henry of Blois, brother of King Stephen,

130 *Winchester Cathedral – the present building dates from after the Norman Conquest. The Anglo-Saxon cathedral was on the near side of the nave*

131 *Wolvesey Palace – the residence of the medieval bishops of Winchester with Winchester College (top left) and the cathedral to the right*

132 *The medieval hospital of St Cross, south of Winchester*

for poor old men (**132**). Their chapel is like a huge cruciform church and dates from the twelfth and thirteenth centuries. The rows of small houses with prominent chimneys are fifteenth-century in date and include a communal dining hall and a gatehouse. Few places in England have so much surviving fabric of the Church in all its manifestations still remaining from the Middle Ages as Winchester and still forming part of the modern landscape.

Further reading

Tom Beaumont James, *Winchester*, Batsford/English Heritage 1997

12

YORK

The third of the historic city studies looks at York. York is one of the few places which looks and feels historic with its Minster, castle, city walls, old churches and myriad early buildings. There is much that is still standing from the medieval period, but even more of the city is influenced by its Roman, Anglian and Viking past – road and street alignments and patterns of property boundaries.

York was founded as a Roman legionary

133 York, with the Minster (left) and the River Ouse (right) looking south-east

fortress, on a higher, level area of gravel between the rivers Ouse and Foss, in the middle of the wide flat Vale of York where many rivers come together before they empty into the Humber. It was a very sound strategic decision by some unknown Roman general (**133**). The outline of the legionary fortress is preserved under some of the city walls and there is at least one large standing fragment in the Multangular Tower (**134**). But the main legacy is in the

east/west alignments of Roman roads running across the fort and in from the south which have survived as streets still in use.

When Christianity came to York with the missionary Paulinus in the early seventh century he seems to have built a church in the fortress in which the local king Edwin could be baptised (in 627) and which could form a mission station. This mission failed as Edwin died in 633 and Paulinus returned to southern England. Nothing of this church has been found, but excavations under the Minster have revealed a long history of occupation in the post-Roman centuries, including reuse of the Roman headquarters building, a developing cemetery and the various earlier churches on the site. The present orientation of the Minster building which all dates to after 1100 (**135**) is on the correct east/west alignment: earlier churches are more likely to have been orientated on the

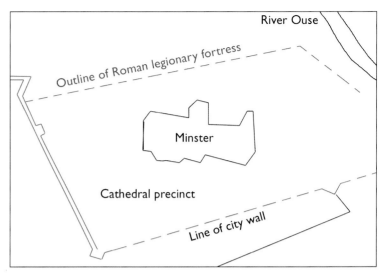

134 (Above) *The Multangular Tower, part Roman (left centre) surviving from the legionary fortress defences*

135 and **plan** (Right and above right) *The Minster and its precinct within the area of the Roman legionary fortress. The medieval town wall and the River Ouse can be seen*

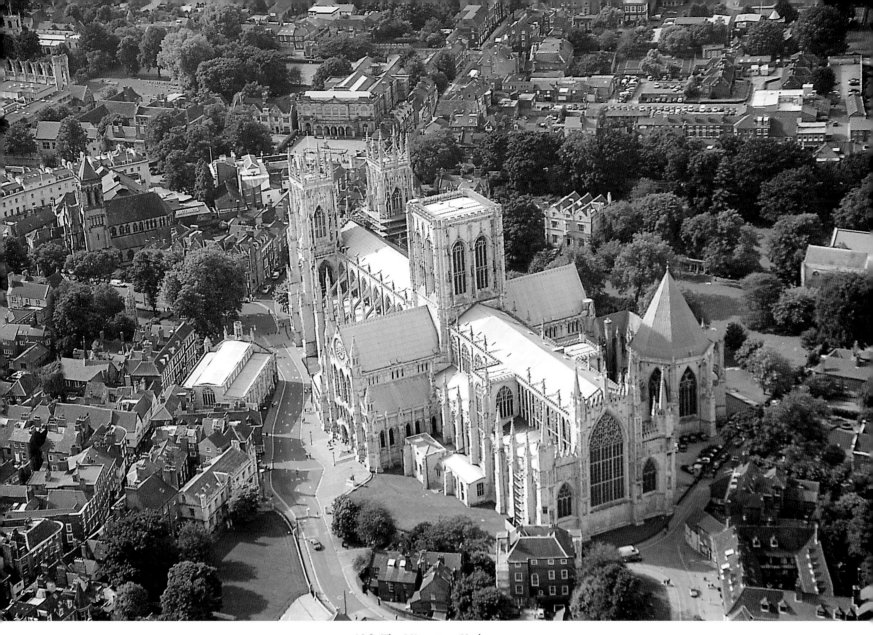

136 *The Minster at York*

Roman fort buildings (**135**). At most times the Minster has been the base for a number of secular (that is not monastic) clergy. It was made a cathedral early on to serve the people of the kingdom of Deira (roughly old Yorkshire) but became the seat of an archbishop – the only other one in England after Canterbury – in 735.

The open space of the Minster precinct shows up well from the air, a green space within a sea of red roofs. In this area were the canon's houses, college and vicar's buildings and several churches. It would always have been a separate and exclusive part of the city – a religious enclave – and as we have seen there are many such examples.

137 (Above) *Clifford's Tower, the keep on top of the Norman motte*

138 (Right) *The main Norman castle at York – Clifford's Tower on the motte, with later buildings in the bailey in the foreground*

With the coming of William the Conqueror and the Normans in 1066 much continued as before at York. But William's hold on the crown was not secure for many years. As elsewhere he built castles, though at York he built two, both of the motte and bailey type. The main one has the well-preserved (but later) Clifford's Tower (**137**) sitting on the top of the Norman motte, with the adjacent bailey now somewhat obscured by later buildings which house a museum (**138**). The other is the less obvious and far less well-known Baile Hill, where a motte remains covered in trees (**139**), but the bailey is built over and obscured. These were placed to defend the approaches to the city up the rivers, rather than from inland, as shown on figure **140** where the Clifford's Tower castle can be seen between the two rivers overlooking their confluence.

During the Middle Ages much of the area of the city was developed for the precincts of newly founded monasteries. These included a very large and early founded

139 (Above) *The other Norman castle at York – on the other side of the Ouse – the motte at Baile Hill (in trees)*

140 (Right) *This view shows how the main castle was built at the confluence of the two rivers at York: the Ouse (left) and the Foss (right)*

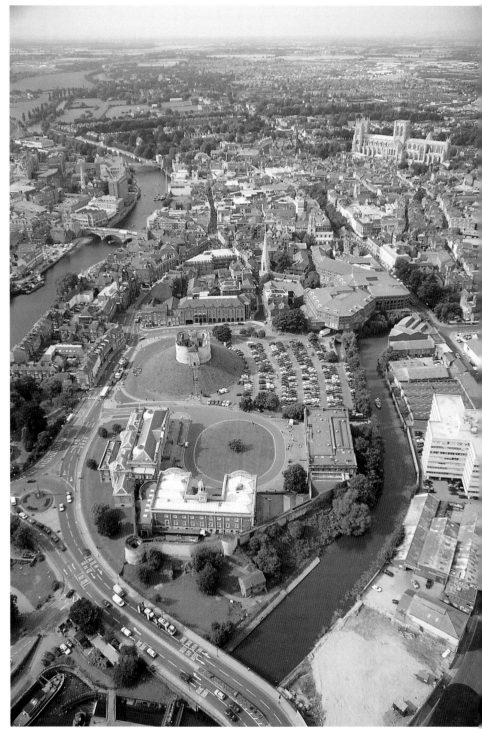

hospital of St Leonards in the corner of the Roman fort, but the most extensive, and arguably the most important historically, was St Mary's Benedictine Abbey built just outside the city walls on the north-west side (**141**). There may have been an earlier religious community here and indeed there might also have been an early royal residence in an enclosure; the church of St Olave also suggests some Danish connection. The present abbey was begun in 1088-9 though the surviving impressive ruins date to a later time (**142**). Perhaps the most important event in its history occurred when thirteen of the monks left in 1132 and, wishing to follow a more austere life, were eventually settled at Fountains. Here they joined the Cistercian order and became part of the expansion of the new monastic orders from the continent into this country in the twelfth century. The great abbey of Fountains in Yorkshire was the result.

141 (Above)
St Mary's Abbey, north of the city, just beyond the city wall. St Leonard's Hospital occupied the lower half of the picture

142 (Right)
The ruins of the abbey church of St Mary's; St Olave's Church is top right

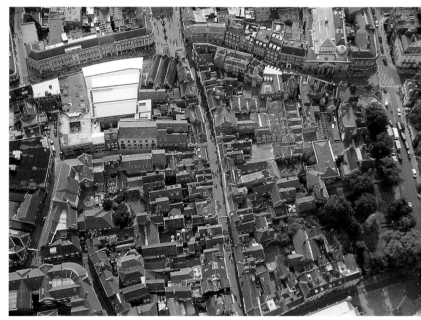

143, 144 (Top and above) *Walmgate – part of the densely built-up area of York inside the walls. Many of these buildings are four to five hundred years old*

145 *Walmgate – many of the properties preserve medieval and probably earlier land boundaries. In the centre is the church of St Denys*

146 *The new Lendal Bridge and road built 1861-3 at the north end of the city. In the centre is St Leonard's Hospital; left of centre the Multangular Tower*

147 (Left) *The main station at York on the North Eastern Railway, dating partly from 1840-2 but mainly 1877. The River Ouse, with Lendal Bridge (left) in the foreground*

148 (Above) *The Royal Station Hotel of 1877-8*

Much of the townscape of York however is made up of the ordinary buildings, yards and gardens of the townsfolk engaged in trade and commerce over the ages (**144**). Though not evident from the air many of the present buildings are medieval in origin. Even more significant, much of the town's landscape preserves the alignments of properties and lanes from the early medieval period – so that even though the fabric is later, the underlying plan structure preserves a much earlier pattern (**143, 145**).

To survive, no town or city can remain static and at York there is plenty of evidence of change and development in the townscape in more recent times. Several new bridges were built crossing the River Ouse (**146**) and a number of new roads were cut through the medieval properties in the nineteenth century to ease access between parts of the town inside the city walls. But the most dramatic change to the townscape came in the nineteenth century with the building of the railway (**147**). The vast areas occupied by tracks, station and yards are almost as large as the medieval city. Not only was the architecture of the railways a totally new aspect of the landscape but they generated other dramatically new developments such as the vast hotels that frequently stood alongside the stations (**148**).

Further reading

Richard Hall, *York*, Batsford/English Heritage 1996

13

WELLS, SOMERSET

Wells has a rather different history to the other three historic cities and it is reflected in its topography. It was never a Roman fort or a tribal capital as far as is known, and there is no substantial Roman city under the present buildings and streets. It only became the seat of a bishop in 909 in a later phase of creation of diocesan centres. Following the council of London in 1075 Archbishop Lanfranc (of Canterbury) removed cathedral clergy from cathedrals situated in non-urban places in the countryside and moved them to the nearest substantial city or centre of population. Wells can have been no more than a village at this time because the cathedral was moved to Bath in 1090 and placed in the Benedictine abbey there. The church at Wells reverted to its role as a large minster church serving the local population as it had done before 909.

Excavations by Warwick Rodwell have located the early cathedral and church (which began as a late Roman mausoleum) to the east of the later

149 *The main street of Wells*

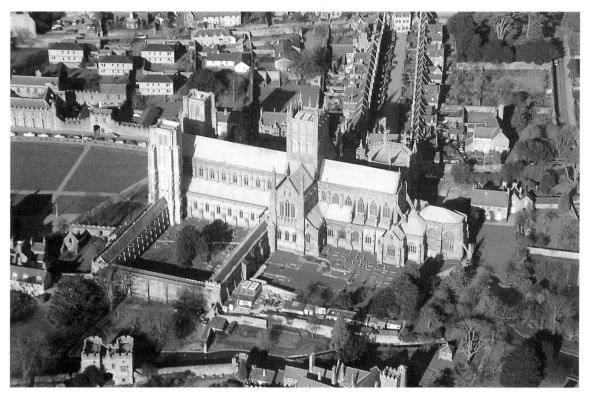

150 *Wells Cathedral and the site of the Anglo-Saxon cathedral (to the right of the cloister) with Vicars Close in the background*

151 *Wells Cathedral with the moated bishop's palace to the left. The early cathedral was between them*

cloister. His excavations showed that the enormous springs, which gave the town its name, were revered at least from the Roman period and provided a focus for a cult centre over several thousand years. These early churches were on a different alignment to the later cathedral and must have lain along the main road that still forms the main street of Wells (**149**). An urban settlement was clearly being developed here by the bishops in the twelfth century, with a market place outside the gates of the minster and rows of burgage properties on each side of the road. Bishop Robert of Lewes (1136-66) had a bishop's throne (or cathedra) at both Bath and Wells and began to rebuild the cathedral at Wells. His successor, Reginald de Bohun, began to build the present cathedral in 1174 (**150**). This was on a different alignment to the earlier cathedral (**151**) and its construction, together with the laying out of a generous area for the precinct,

152 *The bishop's palace with its surrounding moat and the ruined hall of Bishop Burnell*

disrupted the local roads. A bypass was required to go around the north side of the precinct to link the High Street with the road to the east.

This cathedral precinct at Wells is rightly regarded as one of the best surviving collections of medieval buildings of a secular (that is non-monastic) cathedral (**152, 153**). As well as the cathedral, with its cloister and chapter house, there is the moated bishop's palace, with its surviving medieval hall and chambers entered first through a gatehouse off the market place, the fifteenth-century Bishop's Eye, and then an inner gatehouse. The whole moated enclosure is walled around with battlements and towers of the fourteenth century. Alongside the current medieval but heavily restored palace is the ruined great hall of Bishop Burnell (1280-90).

The cathedral was served by canons, rather than monks, and they lived in fine houses many of which survive around the Cathedral Green, to the west of the west front of the cathedral. These were wealthy clerics living off the income of their 'prebends', endowments provided by their various estates. They were not always at the cathedral carrying out their ecclesiastical duties, so these were undertaken for them by 'vicars'. They were provided with a college of houses near the cathedral which were rebuilt in the fifteenth century and survive as the Vicars Close, not so much a medieval street as an elongated medieval cloister. They had a dining hall and a bridge over the street to the cathedral, both of which survive.

Immediately outside the cathedral precinct was the market place with its great conduit where overflow water from the springs was supplied to the town's people. The market tolls were an important source of income for the bishops. Around 1450 Bishop Bekynton built a row of houses and shops, the 'Nova Opera', on the north side of

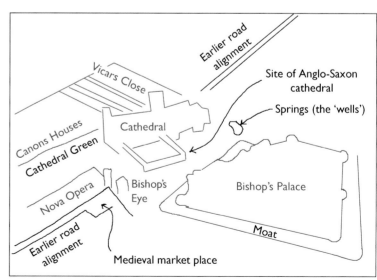

153 and **plan** *The bishop's palace with the cathedral to the north*

the market place, and these can still be seen albeit in altered form.

Unlike the other historic cities discussed here not much is known of the archaeology underground at Wells. There has been little disfiguring redevelopment and so few excavations have been carried out. Much of the medieval townscape is still there and in use, not just in the buildings but in the layout of the streets and lanes and in the pattern of the urban properties which form the 'grain' of the place.

The archaeology of medieval Wells is still there in the ground under the buildings!

Further reading

Warwick Rodwell, *Wells Cathedral: Excavations and Structural Studies* 1978-93, English Heritage London 2001

14

BRIDGNORTH, SHROPSHIRE

Bridgnorth is one of those smaller towns of medieval foundation which is not only a gem today, surviving largely intact, but for which the history is very clearly represented from the air in the townscape. The place-name helps unravel the history of the town. As the name suggests there was a bridge here. It lay some way to the north of Quatford (the main Saxon centre) where there had been a bridge, a burh (a Saxon fortified town), church and castle. What we see at Bridgnorth is a transfer of all this to a new site by the new Norman owner, Robert of Belesme, earl of Shrewsbury. This all happened after around 1100.

We can see that the Earl selected a high southward-facing spur in the Severn valley on the west bank of the river (**154**). On the end of this he built a castle and probably a small borough, which would have been probably no more than an additional enclosure adjacent to the castle itself in which the retainers could live. But as we have already seen elsewhere, in Bridgnorth the present topography – the layout of the place – displays its history.

154 *The spur selected as the site for Bridgnorth with the River Severn (viewed from the north). The castle is at the far end, with the church of St Leonard in the foreground*

It is possible that there might have been a pre-existing hillfort on this promontory – it is such an obviously defensible spot. Rather more likely is that the present church of St Leonard was there in some form. The circular layout of the churchyard is not what we would expect from a church and graveyard laid out along with a new medieval town. Rather it would fit with a much earlier church in a circular yard originally surrounded by countryside, which was later incorporated into the defensive circuit as we shall see. There is no definite evidence for this suggestion so it must remain unproven until the opportunity for excavations arises.

There is a marked difference in the layout of the one end of the town to the other. Such differences in topographical layout are used by scholars to suggest successive stages of development. In this case we know that the castle stood in a roughly triangular point on the end of the peninsula (**155**). The leaning Norman keep remains – an attempt was made to blow it up in the seventeenth-century English Civil War – together with the former castle chapel, now the rebuilt church of St Mary Magdalene. Adjacent to this is the horseshoe-shaped layout of roads lined with fine eighteenth- and nineteenth-century buildings. These are linked to the wide market street via a narrow lane. It is difficult to appreciate this from the air but the land on each side of this lane drops away steeply as if the peninsula is 'pinched' at this point. Lanes go off, in one case to the valley west of the castle, but in the other towards the bridge below. It has been suggested that the defences of the castle and the early borough came through this point and there is a tradition of a gatehouse hereabouts.

Perhaps the whole of the end of this spur was originally selected for the castle above the river and the bridge. At some stage a small settlement could have been carved out of the outer bailey and properties laid out there. Certainly

155 *The area of the castle and probable early borough on the promontory at Bridgnorth*

156 *The medieval market place with the later market hall and the rebuilt town gate. On either side is the pattern of medieval burgages*

from the air it looks as if 'burgages' or town properties were laid out and their successor town properties occupy much of this area now.

The other half of the town is much more like a typical medieval planted and planned town (**156**). It has a central

wide rectangular market place now occupied by a successor to the medieval covered market hall. This wide space would have been used to accommodate the markets held each week – it is now mainly a car park. It was wide enough for the pens for cattle and sheep which would have been brought into the town to be sold on. On each side of this wide space there are the clear signs of the burgage properties in this part of the town. These are long strip-like plots of land with relatively narrow frontages to the street so that everyone can have access to the passing trade. While all the buildings look post-medieval in date, some almost certainly encase earlier structures, masked by later fashionable camouflage to give the impression of owners keeping up to date with architectural innovations. Rows of buildings run back down the plots, often later cottages or outbuildings, kitchens and stores serving the main house on the street frontage.

Bridgnorth was a walled town with gates in the Middle Ages. It was located on the warlike Welsh border and belonged to a powerful family. It also became wealthy enough through trade and commerce to be able to afford a town wall and several stone gate-towers. The most important of these survives as a much rebuilt North Gate seen at the front of the picture. How this has survived is remarkable as such a narrow gate constricts the access to the town. So often gates such as this in other medieval towns were removed to improve traffic flow in the eighteenth and nineteenth centuries. If the town was poor or off the beaten track in later centuries, or if they survived long enough for antiquarian interest to develop and ensure their preservation, then they might still exist. The latter is probably the case here.

Further reading

Mick Aston & James Bond, *The Landscape of Town*, Sutton Stroud 1976, reprinted 2000

Maurice Beresford, *New Towns of the Middle Ages*, London Lutterworth Press 1967 pp.479-80

15

HENLEY IN ARDEN, WARWICKSHIRE

A study of Henley in Arden also shows the close relationship between a medieval lord, his castle and a new town. Figure **157** shows Beaudesert in Warwickshire from the north. The castle consists of a ringwork (**158**) and several baileys or enclosures draped along a ridge of high land detached from the escarpment off to the left but also visible as wooded slope in the background. Away to the right (west) side of the castle is the medieval new town of Henley in Arden planted long after the castle had been built. The landscape in the foreground has a number of features of interest. Even though this photograph was taken in September and the sun is still relatively high in the sky, there are enough shadows thrown by the various earthworks in the fields to enable us to clearly see lots of traces of earlier activity.

Former fishponds are indicated by the large earthworks of dams and retaining banks and the course of a largely dried-up stream that would have fed them with water. All around,

157 *The castle at Beaudesert with its ringwork (centre) and baileys (right). In the foreground are the earthworks of fishponds and ridge and furrow. Henley in Arden is off to the right*

including on the slopes of the hill with the castle, are traces of ridge and furrow, the corrugated earthworks associated particularly with medieval ploughing. It has been assumed that the fishponds were part of the trappings of the medieval castle, which also included a medieval hunting park, formerly occupying most of the lower half of the picture, as well as a lot of land beyond.

It is not clear why there should be evidence of ploughed land in what was a hunting area. Feasible explanations include the possibility that the ridge and furrow dates from before the park was founded, or after the area had been abandoned for hunting and had reverted back to agriculture. Perhaps such parks were ploughed from time to time and crops taken from them. The fishponds might also not be associated with the castle, though they often were, and they are often found in parks. However, there was a large post-medieval mansion just behind the castle so there remains the possibility that the fishponds were constructed later and were

158 (Above) *The ringwork of the castle under excavation in 2001*

159 and **plan** (Right) *Beaudesert with its castle, church and borough site; in the foreground is the successive medieval new town of Henley with its burgage properties and town chapel*

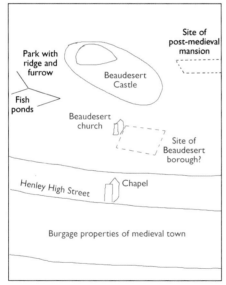

Park with ridge and furrow

Fish ponds

Beaudesert Castle

Site of post-medieval mansion

Beaudesert church

Site of Beaudesert borough?

Henley High Street

Chapel

Burgage properties of medieval town

part of an ordered gentile landscape of leisure for the people of the house. No doubt this also included the abandoned castle site which would have provided a ready-made folly as well as splendid views of the country around, as it still does for the local people.

The documents suggest that the man who built the castle, Thurstan de Montfort, also tried to develop a borough with a market at the base of the castle at Beaudesert, where the very fine Romanesque church is situated today. Whether this was a success or not, by the early thirteenth century a new town was being developed over the stream along the main road heading for Stratford upon Avon (itself a new town founded by the bishops of Worcester in the late twelfth century). Figure **159** shows

the relationship between the castle, church and early centre at Beaudesert and the new medieval town of Henley. The new settlement did not have its own church and graveyard since it was in Wootton Wawen parish and the parish church was several miles away even though Beaudesert church was only up the lane. It was not until 1367 that the bishop of Worcester permitted the inhabitants to have their own town chapel (**160**), which they had to build and pay for, and even then no burial rights were granted. This explains why the chapel even today does not have any graveyard and is hemmed in by town buildings, including the guildhall, on all sides. At least it was handy to the townsfolk being in the centre of the town.

All along the medieval main road, 'burgages' or town properties were laid out, and favourable rents would have been set to attract people to the new speculative urban venture. The planned nature of this development is given away by the regular pattern of the properties and the consistent uniform rear property-line, which bounds the back of the plots.

As at Bridgnorth, most of the buildings along this medieval town street appear to date from later than the Middle Ages, though many of them are timber-framed, it is likely that parts of medieval structures remain to be discovered within the existing buildings.

Further reading

Mick Aston & James Bond, *The Landscape of Towns,* Sutton Stroud 1976, reprinted 2000

Maurice Beresford, *New Towns of the Middle Ages,* London Lutterworth Press 1967 pp.139 and 500

160 *The centre of the new medieval town at Henley in Arden with the market place, chapel and pattern of burgage properties*

16

DESERTED MEDIEVAL VILLAGES

It is no exaggeration to say that the study of landscape archaeology initially grew on the back of the study of deserted villages. As William Hoskins and Maurice Beresford, among others, began to examine the development of the countryside using maps, documents and fieldwork they came across more and more examples of settlements that had disappeared in the past. Many of these had only a ruined church or a single remaining farm together with a sea of surrounding earthworks of what had once been a thriving village community. The fossilization of features such as old hollow ways, earthwork platforms, moated sites, fishponds, village boundary banks and field systems of ridge and furrow, meant that much of the earlier, usually medieval landscape, could be reconstructed with little difficulty.

Wharram Percy in the East Riding of Yorkshire was one of the first of these deserted villages to be recognized – indeed it was never really lost, always known by local

161 *Wharram Percy in Yorkshire with its ruined church, fishpond and in the background the earthworks of the deserted village*

people and marked on early Ordnance Survey maps (**161**). It has been subject to over forty seasons of archaeological excavation so we know a lot about it. Even so, only seven per cent of the area has been fully excavated. All that is left is the ruined medieval church and a row of nineteenth-century cottages, but all around is a vast area of well-preserved earthworks (**162**). These enable us to see the former positions of the medieval longhouses, their farmyards and gardens, the lanes and the boundary of the village and its properties (**163**).

The plan of the original village consisted of a long green, on the side of the valley, with farms along each side. At the north, lower, end was a great manorial enclosure ('the North Manor') (**164**) while at the south was the church. Excavations have shown that the village was probably laid out, planned even, in the late Saxon period, and occupied until the fifteenth century when it was abandoned. Before the village came into existence there

162 (Top) *Wharram Percy – the main area of the village with house sites (centre), some outlined in concrete and their farmyards behind (right)*

163 (Above) *Wharram Percy – the top end of the village with the area of the north manor (top right). The latter has not been excavated but the earthworks have a different plan from those of the village properties*

164 (Right) *Wharram Percy – the earthworks of the north manor area with the main part of the village in the background*

was a scatter of farms in prehistoric, Roman and early Saxon times; after the village was abandoned there were again only a few farms working the former arable farming areas. Lessons from the excavations here seem to be relevant to many villages, surviving and deserted, all over the country.

In the Cotswolds there are a large number of deserted and shrunken villages and hamlets. Many of them never had churches, so they are really hamlets, and quite a lot have not completely disappeared so they are really shrunken rather than deserted. One that demonstrates their history is Manless Town in Brimpsfield (**165**). The earthworks of the village are not very well preserved but lying across them, rather symbolically, is the long rectangular outline of the foundations of the later sheepcote. Here the sheep that replaced the villagers on the site would have been housed and fed in the winter. The strange name refers to the lack of people; the medieval name seems to have been Haywick.

John Rous, a fifteenth-century chantry priest from Guy's Cliff near Warwick, gives us a list of the places he knew had been abandoned in his lifetime and these next sites were on it. He was concerned not surprisingly with the abandoned churches so it is incidental that we learn about abandoned villages. Lower Ditchford village site has very well-preserved earthworks but it has never been excavated (**166**). All that is left is a rebuilt water mill and farm. The course of former village roads and lanes can be seen, as well as the site of a fishpond and the earthwork platforms on which the medieval farm buildings stood. They were probably of turf, timber and thatch as there are no clear stone foundations such as can be seen on upland sites. All around are the corrugations of ridge and furrow, remains of the strips of the medieval common field system (**167**). At Hawling (**168**), by contrast, not only are the farmstead sites clearer, because stone was used in their foundations, but detailed documentary study has shown something of the complex history of the site. This, in fact, is a shrunken village site, as there is still a big village at Hawling.

165 (Top) *Manless Town, Brimpsfield, Gloucestershire – the sheepcote is in the centre of the picture*

166 (Above) *The earthworks of Lower Ditchford village, Gloucestershire*

167 *Ridge and furrow of the common field system near Ditchford in Gloucestershire*

However, amazingly, the area of farm sites and enclosures on the right of the picture was not originally part of Hawling. It was called Roelside in the Middle Ages and belonged to the village of Roel some miles away and is itself now deserted, with a manor house, remains of a chapel and the earthworks of a village street with house sites alongside (**169**). Another good example of a shrunken village is Hampnett (**170**). The few surviving cottages around the spring here give little impression of what the medieval plan of the village was like. The earthworks show that there was originally a large rectangular village green here with the spring at its upper end, presumably supplying the villagers with water. All around is a very regular pattern of properties defined by earthwork banks marking the village properties. The earthworks of house sites can be seen in some of these. All around is a former village boundary bank separating off the closes of the village from the fields with their crops.

Large numbers of these sites have now been identified all over the country. They show us that there were

168 *Hawling in Gloucestershire – the shrunken village earthworks with Roelside (right, in shadow)*

formerly far more places occupied in the landscape and that the places that are still there often were more densely occupied or had a different plan in the past. Most of the evidence remains as earthworks, and of course as archaeology in the ground. There seems to be relatively little detail in the documents about when and how most of these places were deserted. Included here are examples from Wiltshire (**171** Westleaze in Wroughton and **172** Woodhill in Clyffe Pypard), Oxfordshire (**173** Pinkhill in Stanton Harcourt), Somerset (**174** Nether Adber in Mudford) and Yorkshire (**175** High Worsall). In each case there are earthworks remaining indicating the position of roads and lanes, farm sites and boundaries. In a few cases the actual sites of houses or farmsteads can be clearly seen, usually when the foundations are of stone rather than timber or turf.

169 *Roel in Gloucestershire – the site of the village to the left, the manor and chapel to the right*

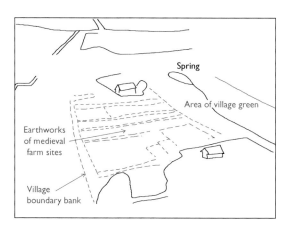

170 and **plan** *Hampnett, Gloucestershire – the shrunken village earthworks around the village green*

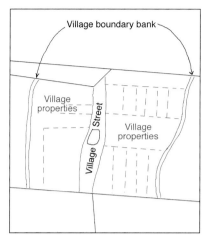

171 and **plan** (Left) *Westleaze in Wroughton, Wiltshire, with its wide village street and other characteristic earthworks*

172 (Below) *Woodhill in Clyffe Pypard, Wiltshire, with a moated site*

It took a long time for archaeologists and historians to realise that deserted medieval settlements existed out in the landscape as we have seen. Part of the reason for this was that the earthwork remains of them were usually thought to be something else (often quarrying or drainage was suggested by farmers) and were thought to be of no significance. Now that they are well understood there may be the occasional suggestion that somewhere is a deserted village when it is something else. Figures 176 and 177 are two views of earthworks at Low Ham in

173 (Above) *Pinkhill in Stanton Harcourt, Oxfordshire, with a mill leat and the River Thames in the background*

174 and **plan** (Right) *Nether Adber in Mudford, Somerset with lanes and house sites*

175 and **plan** (Below) *High Worsall in Yorkshire with the church site in the enclosure (centre), the village green and the house and farm sites; one house site is being excavated*

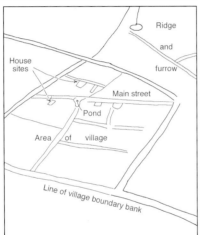

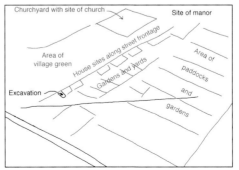

Somerset. When I first saw these I thought, briefly, that they might represent the remains of a village that had stood next to the isolated church that can be seen next to the farm buildings. There is however something odd about these big earthwork platforms and the extremely regular nature of some of the smaller earthworks associated with them. The church is a seventeenth-century chapel rebuilt on a medieval site. A small amount of research in the County Record Office showed that this was the remains, not of a village, which was always on the other side of the church beyond the farm, but of an elaborate series of gardens and landscaping. This was associated with two demolished mansions of the seventeenth and eighteenth centuries. Other earthworks in the adjacent fields helped to clarify the details of their history and development. As usual it is an appreciation of the context of the earthworks, and the history from maps and documents if these are available, which needs to follow the view from the air if the story of a bit of landscape is to be adequately explained.

177 Low Ham, Somerset – the extensive terraces and platforms of the garden earthworks south of the church

176 Low Ham, Somerset – the church (right centre) next to the site of the mansion (bottom right) with the earthworks of the gardens (left)

Further reading

Michael Aston, David Austin & Christopher Dyer (eds), *The Rural Settlements of Medieval England: Studies dedicated to Maurice Beresford and John Hurst*, Basil Blackwell Oxford 1989

Maurice Beresford, *The Lost Villages of England*, Lutterworth 1954 (and later editions)

Maurice Beresford & John Hurst, *Wharram Percy Deserted Medieval Village*, Batsford/English Heritage 1990

Richard Muir, *The Lost Villages of Britain,* Michael Joseph London 1982

Christopher Taylor, *Village and Farmstead: A History of Rural Settlement in England*, George Philip London 1983

17

COALBROOKDALE & IRONBRIDGE, SHROPSHIRE

It is sometimes difficult for us to fully appreciate the landscapes of industrialization for the value they have to our understanding of the past. For holidays, most of us born and brought up in industrial towns would leave these areas as fast as possible to get to the coast or picturesque uplands. But Britain is unique as the home of the Industrial Revolution and so these early industrial landscapes are important on a world scale. It is therefore only right that some of them should be preserved for future generations to visit, as examples of the industrialization process and what it meant to the people at the time.

The generally peaceful pastoral view of the Severn valley in Shropshire (**178**) belies the former importance of the area as the birthplace of the Industrial Revolution. Admittedly the power station with its cooling towers shows something other than rural, but most of what

178 *The Severn valley above Ironbridge*

can be seen in this picture suggests idyllic English countryside. The river Severn here wanders across its flood plain in great meanders; on the right is the site of Buildwas Abbey, a Cistercian twelfth-century foundation which was involved in farming and developing the area in the early Middle Ages.

In the background however is an odd geomorphological feature, the Ironbridge Gorge (**179**). Here, because of the disruption caused to the natural flow of the drainage in the area at the end of the last Ice Age, the river now flows straight through a deep gorge. The complex geology of the area was exposed in the sides of the gorge and was one of the factors that contributed to the early industrial importance of the Ironbridge area.

Off the main river valley on the north side lies Coalbrookdale (**180**). This is another steep-sided valley with a stream in the bottom. Like many others in this area the

111

power from this stream was harnessed to drive mills built at intervals along the valley bottom. These were subsequently rebuilt and enlarged so that large areas of the valley are now occupied by the successors to these mills – factories of various sorts (**181**).

Before the factories the landscape would have looked much more rural. Just upstream from Ironbridge at Leighton something of this landscape can still be seen. Figure **182** shows Leighton with the mass of the Wrekin beyond, a prominent hill with an Iron Age hillfort on the top which was probably the local tribal strongpoint of the Cornovii tribe in the pre-Roman period. Running down from this is a series of wooded valleys with streams, one of which would have driven a mill in Leighton itself. It is difficult to appreciate the site of this as the pond has been filled in and the waterwheel and other parts of the machinery have now been covered by the buildings of the public house. However, recent excavations in 2001 have shown (**183**) that in the seventeenth century there was a charcoal-fired blast furnace here, powered by bellows, driven by a water wheel, that provided the blasts of air into the furnace. This produced iron, which among other things was used to make cannonballs in the English Civil War. The fuel used was charcoal produced from the extensive woodlands around which must have been carefully managed to produce a continuous supply of poles and small timber to be made into charcoal.

Furnaces elsewhere in this region were also fired with charcoal until the early eighteenth century. It is difficult to imagine now how important a fuel charcoal was in earlier times. Any process requiring heat was likely to be fired

179 (Left) *The Ironbridge Gorge from the west*

Opposite
180 (Above left) *The Coalbrookdale valley*

181 (Left) *The Coalbrookdale valley with Darby's furnace (centre)*

182 (Right) *Leighton, site of an early iron furnace, with the Wrekin beyond*

183 *Leighton – the public house on the site of the charcoal-fired blast furnace and the excavations of 2001*

with charcoal that had first to be produced from wood in clamps set up by itinerant charcoal burners in the woods. Lots of people would have been engaged in this process and it must have gone on apace since at least the Bronze Age. Only in a few parts of the country was coal appreciated as a fuel. In the Middle Ages coal was shipped from north-east England to London (where it was known as 'seacoal') and many monasteries had coal deposits on their lands which were occasionally and sporadically worked on a relatively small scale. Coal was even used occasionally in the Roman period. But it was not until the eighteenth century that it became the most widely used fuel. And then it was as coke, a fuel derived from coal by 'cooking' it and driving off the gases.

The furnace at Leighton never seems to have been converted from charcoal to coke power and so it remained as a relic of earlier technology. Its owners presumably never saw the necessity to invest in the new process.

Down at Coalbrookdale, however, a momentous change took place in the early eighteenth century. While all the local conditions were the same as at Leighton, different ownership meant that changes were carried out. Abraham Darby (the first, as there were others later with the same name, 1678-1717) and his successors developed the use of coke to fire their furnaces, enabling greater production of pig iron at their sites. This was first employed at Coalbrookdale in 1709 though there had been earlier experimental attempts with copper at Bristol. Not for the first time the experimentation of an individual changed the local and then the national circumstances.

The site of these innovations was the furnace in Coalbrookdale (**184**) which is shown alongside later ruins. The actual furnace is under the rather incongruous tent-shaped structure, now one of the main features of the World Heritage Site here. As we have seen the area is now much more built up than it would have been then, but something of the scattered nature of the houses, cottages and workshops can still be seen in this area. These early industrial processes produced a messy scattered sort of landscape with no apparent plan nor reason to it. This is equally true of many of the other early industrial areas of the British Isles.

The local availability of iron ore, coal and other minerals such as limestone (for use as the flux in iron smelting), together with water power from the streams to drive the bellows of the blast furnaces, were important prerequisites for the success of the industry. Equally important were good transport facilities, by water up and down the River Severn, and the adoption of innovations by members of the local families. These factors quickly established and developed this area as the prime mover to industrialization in the eighteenth century. Before this time, goods had been individually produced by craftsmen in workshops. As the century developed larger groups of workers in factories produced goods not only on a larger

184 *Abraham Darby's coke-fired furnace at Coalbrookdale (under the tent-like building)*

scale but also more uniformly – mass production had begun. While the process speeded up in the eighteenth century it was clearly being developed in the seventeenth century. In the Ironbridge area a whole range of products were later developed ranging from iron goods to pottery and porcelain, bricks and tiles, clay tobacco pipes and various chemicals.

The area of course gets its name from the iron bridge put up in 1779 and opened in 1781 across the River Severn (**185**). This was an innovation at the time, a bridge made of cast iron sections and then put together rather as if it had been made of wood. It showed just what could be achieved if enough iron could be produced in the more efficient furnaces. Figure **186** shows clearly how built up and town-like the area had become by 1800. There is a church, market place and hotel as well as rows of cottages and workers' housing. Even today most people do not find

186 *The town of Ironbridge on the north side of the river*

these industrial landscapes attractive, preferring the rural idyll of rolling fields and downland. But they represent the beginning of the changes which eventually led to the post-industrial economy which we enjoy today, and as such are themselves fossils of an earlier economy.

Postscript

It is surprising how many areas of early industrialization are associated with medieval monasteries, often of the Cistercian order. Thus there is Buildwas at Ironbridge, Kirkstall at Leeds, Fountains with land all over Yorkshire, Neath, Margam and Tintern in South Wales, and so on. We know that many of these sites had mills and forges but it is not clear how heavily they were engaged in industrialization. Such activities seem to be poorly documented and there is only limited archaeological evidence so far. Could it be that the developments of the seventeenth and eighteenth centuries which are well documented and for which we can see the physical evidence, were in fact based on moves towards greater industrial activity by many of the monastic houses in the fifteenth and sixteenth centuries?

Further reading

Catherine Clark, *Ironbridge Gorge*, Batsford/English Heritage 1993
Richard Hayman & Wendy Horton, *Ironbridge: History and Guide*,
Tempus Stroud 1999

18

BLAENAVON, SOUTH WALES

Despite the relatively unattractive appearance of the Blaenavon area (**187**) it is now rightly, like Ironbridge, a World Heritage site. Ironically, visitors came to the area in the early nineteenth century and recorded it in paintings and drawings just because it was an industrial area full of activity and they were impressed with such commercial ventures and its productivity.

187 *General view across the reclaimed industrial landscape*

Coal and iron had been mined and extracted here on a small scale for many years before the late eighteenth century and many of the small pits and quarries still to be seen in the area may reflect this earlier activity. But it was the foundation of furnaces for iron making in 1787 that began the intensive development of this landscape (**189**). The site was chosen by Thomas Hill, a banker from Stourbridge, and Benjamin

If the Ironbridge area shows some of the aspects of the early developments in iron working then Blaenavon illustrates later developments in the industry. Figure **188** shows the area today with the edge of the town of Blaenavon, the furnaces at the Cadw-Welsh Historic monuments site, reclaimed areas with playing fields, and the moorland on the uplands beyond. This only gives a partial impression of what this landscape was like at the height of industrial activity in the middle of the nineteenth century. It has been 'tidied up' as industrial activity ceased and 'sanitised' by removing much of the evidence seen up until recently as derelict land.

Pratt from Oldswinford, near Stourbridge. A third partner was Thomas Hopkins from Rugeley. All three were from the West Midlands and, as was appropriate at the time, they all had interests in other industrial activities such as fireclay, canals and forges.

There have been many later additions and alterations to the Blaenavon ironworks, and much has been demolished, but the basic outlines are still clear. Several furnaces were built in the side of a small valley by cutting back the hillside. Coal was made into coke in large covered mounds and the iron weathered and roasted, to drive out impurities, on the

hillside above. The raw materials of coal and iron were derived from mining in the hills nearby and brought down in an elaborate series of tramways. Over the years, and particularly when the extraction was on a very large scale in the nineteenth century, vast areas of waste tip heaps developed burying the natural hillside and totally altering the original topography. The finger-like pattern of these dumps is much more obvious from the air (**190**).

The furnaces were loaded from above and the waste slag and the molten iron, called pig iron, tapped off into cast houses below (now with new roofs). The pig iron was taken away on a tramway to be forged into wrought iron at the forge down the Afon valley at Cwmavon (**191**) or taken down the valley to the Monmouth canal and out to the docks at Newport. An innovation was that, rather than using water power to drive the bellows which provided the blast of air to the furnace, a Boulton and Watt steam engine was introduced. This used a local water supply, but could also be powered by the abundant local coal sources.

Because the furnaces at Blaenavon were constructed on the side of an unoccupied mountain, housing and later

188 The furnaces in Blaenavon, foreground left, with the uplands in the background

189 The Blaenavon ironworks with the furnaces (top left) and the workers' housing, Stack Square (bottom right)

190 *The tips and dumps of waste material on the hills behind Blaenavon*

191 *Cwmavon, site of the early forge in the Afon valley*

192 *The other side of the mountain with the early tramways remaining as earthworks – the horizontal terraces*

shops, churches and a school had to be provided for the workers. Stack Square (**189**) is the only early group of workers housing to remain. It was built in 1789-92. By 1810 two more furnaces had been built at Blaenavon together with another steam engine.

After 1815 a later Thomas Hill completely altered the arrangements and many elements of the landscape relate to this phase. He had a tunnel cut, over a mile long, through the mountain to the valleys south of Abergavenny. Tramways were then employed not only to bring limestone from local quarries around the slopes to Blaenavon – limestone was an essential flux in the process of iron production – but also to take the pig iron to a new forge built at Garnddyris. Pig iron and forged iron could then be taken on, around the contours of Blorenge mountain, to an inclined plain above Llanfoist which ran down to the Monmouthshire and Brecon canal. Figure **192** shows the other side of the mountain from Blaenavon where the tunnel was and the lines of the tramways; small limestone quarries can be seen on the slopes. Figure **193** shows the

193 *Earthworks marking the site of the forge at Garnddyris*

194 *Tramways around the mountain (top left) with the inclined plain (right) and the canal (bottom right)*

earthworks at the site of the Garnddyris forge site, which was shut down in 1861, together with the line of the tramway, which was also abandoned at the same time. The course of this tramway goes off round the mountain to the inclined plain above the canal (**193**). On this side of the mountain, in the much more rural surroundings of fields and woods, the landscape is included in the Brecon Beacons National Park. This present rural scene belies, as we have seen, the frantic industrial activity that went on here two hundred years ago. It reminds us that landscapes which we think of as rural and tranquil could have been quite different not so very long ago.

Further reading

Jeremy Knight, *Blaenavon Ironworks: a Bicentennial Guide*, Cadw Welsh Historic Monuments 1989

19

THE GREAT HOUSES

The next few examples demonstrate just how dramatic changes could be with the wholesale removal of earlier agricultural landscapes and the creation of totally new 'landscapes of pleasure'.

Castle Howard, in the North Riding of Yorkshire, is not only a very fine example of a great palatial baroque mansion, it also demonstrates the extinction of one landscape and the creation of a totally different one. The earlier landscape consisted of the village of *Henderskelfe* with its common fields and closes. Adjacent to it was Ray Wood and this was retained in the new landscape. In the middle of the village was the 'castle' of the place name; in fact it was rather more like a fortified manor house. By the end of the seventeenth century the owner of this castle, probably the first or second Lord Carlisle, had begun to encroach on the village roads and closes in order to create something of the newly fashionable gardens and a park thought desirable at the time. This might have been as far as it went without total control of the landscape, the availability of a lot of wealth and the strong desire to create an impressive fashionable statement in the landscape by the third Earl of Carlisle.

From the early 1700s the village was removed, the old castle demolished and the creation of the new landscape

195 *Castle Howard from the west with Ray Wood beyond. The earlier 'castle' was on the site of the circular garden*

196 *Castle Howard from the north*

with its vast mansion begun. Figure **195** shows the site of the village of *Henderskelfe* which ran more or less along the line of the straight gravel path, with farms and cottages in the area at the front of the picture where there is an archaeological evaluation trench. The village main road and other houses ran off to the right under the later kitchen garden. The castle was situated more or less where the circular path is in front of the house. Ray Wood

is in the background. At this date it is very unlikely that the villagers were just cast out to wander and find employment elsewhere. Although we do not know in detail what happened to them, in all probability they were moved to one of the adjacent villages, Bulmer, Coneysthorpe and Welburn, which still survive today and have become estate villages. A big house and a large estate here would in any case have needed an army of craftsmen, gardeners and workers concerned with the maintenance of the fabric and the running of the house.

The big house was begun in 1700 following the designs of Vanbrugh, an army officer with no experience of architecture, who had begun to develop a career as a dramatist. It is impossible to imagine anything like this happening today. Nicholas Hawksmoor, who had been Sir Christopher Wren's clerk of works since 1679, was soon also involved, however, and he did know about building.

The original design consisted of the central block, the eastern or kitchen wing in the background, and a western wing which would have matched the eastern but was never built. The great dome over the central block, which is such a distinctive feature of Castle Howard, was added a few years later in 1706. The west wing was finally built to a different design in the 1750s. To the west of that it was intended to build the stables but in the end these were not built until the 1780s and then were positioned much further to the west beyond the village site.

From about 1712 when the kitchen wing was finished the attention of the architect and owner turned to the creation of the landscape around the house, where formerly there had been fields and farmland. The vast kitchen garden (**197**) with its own gardener's house in the middle designed by Vanbrugh was built in the early 1700s. Much of it covers the village of *Henderskelfe* and excavations in 2002 found traces of the seventeenth-century houses. The chimney marks the central heating system for glass houses (now removed) in which exotic fruits like peaches and oranges would have been grown. The stable block, a mini-mansion in its own right, is nearby. It was built in 1781-4 by the architect John Carr.

Much of the landscape beyond these areas but close to the house was, over the eighteenth century, dramatically changed. Rivers were dammed to form large lakes, roads were diverted and straight rides created, and the parkland was peppered with follies and monuments. The road to the west which runs dead straight for seven kilometres (nearly five miles) must have been made around 1714 to 1719 (**198**) since the obelisk (**199**), built to commemorate the building of the house and the planting of the plantations, was built in 1714. The various gates and monuments along it date from 1719 onwards. Perhaps the finest piece of created landscape lies to the south of the house. The South Lake was begun before Vanbrugh died in 1726. Beyond it (**200**) can be seen the bridge of 1744 and the fantastic mausoleum designed by Nicholas Hawksmoor but not built until 1731-42 (**201**).

To the south of the house the garden is more formal. It looks towards a monumental pyramid (**202**) built in 1728 to celebrate the Howard's acquisition of the estate before 1639. In the centre of the south garden (**203**),

197 *The kitchen garden at Castle Howard, much of which covers the site of* Henderskelfe *village*

Opposite
198 (Above left) *The avenue at Castle Howard*

199 (Below left) *The obelisk with Castle Howard in the background*

200 (Above right) *The South Lake, bridge and mausoleum at Castle Howard*

201 (Below right) *The mausoleum at Castle Howard*

202 *The pyramid at Castle Howard*

203 *The south garden at Castle Howard from the south*

The British landscape is dotted with large numbers of these stately homes and parks, not usually as big and impressive as Castle Howard, often not as well documented, and many not as well maintained. And yet they have all been planned, laid out and landscaped in relatively recent times, over the last four hundred years, from landscapes that had been well farmed and settled for hundreds of years beforehand. Included here for comparison are Blenheim Palace, near Woodstock in Oxfordshire, Bowood and Longleat in Wiltshire, and Cirencester Park in Gloucestershire.

Blenheim Palace was built, again to the designs of John Vanbrugh, following the victory over the French army of Louis XIV by John Churchill, Duke of Marlborough, in 1704. It was in effect a national monument given to him by Queen Anne, rather than just a residence for the family. The scale of the building, like at Castle Howard, was vast (**204**) with the hall, principal apartments and residential

204 *Blenheim Palace*

reflecting the rather more formal designs of nineteenth-century gardens, is a large fountain with a statue of Atlas carrying the globe. This emphasises the long period over which these designed landscapes were developed. Beyond is the vast North or Great Lake of 90 acres added in 1798-1800.

205 *Blenheim Palace with New Woodstock in the background*

206 *The park with bridge, column and planting next to Blenheim Palace*

block in the centre, with courts to either side – Kitchen Court in the background and Stable Court with the nearby nineteenth-century gardens in the foreground. Unlike Castle Howard, there had been a medieval park here, next to a royal residence, Woodstock Palace. On the edge of the park a new town had been built in the 1100s, New Woodstock, to house and service the visitors to this palace (205). The site of the palace is known; it was on a prominent mound overlooking fishponds and a mill site, now covered by the late eighteenth-century lakes. From before the medieval park was created, extended and developed, traces of earlier prehistoric and Roman landscapes survive as earthworks within the park. The full development of this landscape park is extremely complex but has been disentangled by, among others, James Bond. Figure 206 shows the palace, Vanbrugh's Grand Bridge of 1716 onwards and the Column of Victory of 1727-30. All around are the elaborate planting schemes of trees in the park. The very formal avenue of lime trees, though replanted, is a feature from Vanbrugh's time, though with later modifications. The more informal clumps of trees dotted around the landscape with linear shelter belts around the edges date to the time of Lancelot 'Capability' Brown in the 1760s. He also created the vast serpentine lakes thus flooding the bottom half of Vanbrugh's bridge.

The main house at Bowood, which had been developed by Orlando Bridgeman, Robert Adam and Henry Keene in the middle of the eighteenth century, was demolished in 1955-6, a common fate for hundreds of big houses of this period. All that is left, though it is vast, is the extensive stable block around two courts, built by Henry Keene for the first Earl of Shelbourne (207). It was added to by Robert Adam in 1769-70. Rather like at Blenheim, the more formal terraced gardens to the south (foreground) and east (right) of the house were added in the nineteenth century. Beyond can be seen the extensive kitchen gardens. Over 1,000 acres of gardens and landscaping lie around the house, the work of successively Hamilton (of

Pains Hill, Surrey), Capability Brown in 1761-8, and Humphrey Repton. It has a large lake (**208**) where there is a cascade, and there is a mausoleum designed by Robert Adam and completed 1765.

No villages are known to have been displaced by the construction of the vast landscape project at Bowood; indeed the area seems to have been mainly royal forest in the

207 (Left) *The vast stable blocks at Bowood*

208 (Top) *Bowood with its lake and landscaping*

209 (Above) *Derry Hill, one of the estate villages of Bowood*

210 (Left) *Sandy Lane estate village near Bowood*

211 (Above) *Longleat House and stables, with the lake beyond*

Longleat House of the 1560s and 1570s (**211**) replaced a small and insignificant Augustinian priory of St Radegund that was virtually defunct even before the dissolution of the monasteries put an end to it. This area, the north end of the former extensive forest of Selwood, was not heavily settled in the Middle Ages and it is likely that the priory was surrounded by extensive areas of woodland while it was in existence. It is still a very extensive area of woodland and plantations today.

The house was built for the Thynne family, some of the nouveau riche of the sixteenth century who profited from the destruction of the monastic houses and the confiscation of their lands. As well as the house there are the usual extensive outbuildings, including the early nineteenth-century stables (by Sir Jeffry Wyatville) and to the north of the house the orangery with a garden. There must have been extensive formal gardens at Longleat but these were swept aside by Capability Brown in 1757-62 and by

Middle Ages, but there are several estate villages around the periphery of the park. Derry Hill (**209**), of neo-Tudor housing with the Lansdowne Arms, lies outside the Golden Gates, which were designed by Barry with an Italianate turret in the middle of the nineteenth century. Sandy Lane (**210**) is a complete chocolate-box-lid pastiche of 'merrie England' with its thatched cottages, roses and kitchen gardens.

212 *Longleat House in its landscaped park*

Humphrey Repton in the early 1800s (**212**). The open landscape with plantations and clumps of trees with the lakes and garden features date from these episodes.

Cirencester Park presents something of a contrast being right next to a large town. Indeed, the big house is only just outside the urban area, and a few hundred yards from the parish church and the site of the large medieval abbey (**213**). It is separated from the town by a high wall and enormous yew hedge. The house was built in 1714-18 by Allen the first Lord Bathurst, probably on the site of an earlier manor house. He was a friend and patron of Alexander Pope, the poet and arbiter of taste and fashion in the eighteenth century. It seems to have been Pope and

other friends who advised Lord Bathurst on the development of the enormous park, which stretches away to the west for many miles, and which, with its avenues and straight planting, was rather out of fashion by the time it was completed in 1775.

In some respects the development of these great houses and their extensive landscaped estates had the greatest impact of almost any major landscape change on the villages and fields they replaced. Often, as we have seen, relict features are left behind in the landscape from previous activity. Nobody could be bothered in effect to wipe the slate completely clean before embarking on some new activity. But on these estates there is total

213 *Cirencester Park with the mansion, on the edge of the town of Cirencester*

replacement of roads, fields and buildings, together with damming of streams and planting of vast areas of new trees. Completely new landscapes were created in which the local inhabitants must have felt very disorientated, at least to begin with. Excavation at sites such as Castle Howard has also shown how thoroughly the villagers' houses and property boundaries were removed, so making it impossible for anyone to ever come back and even locate where their house formerly stood.

And yet these houses and estates are as much a reflection of the activities of these country people in the landscape as they are of the lords that owned them. While we usually know a lot about the landowner and the architects he employed, and from the documents we can learn when a particular lake was dammed or folly created, we seldom know the names or anything of the lives of the people who did the work on the ground. Such landscapes are as much a memorial to the vast armies of quarrymen, woodmen, ditch diggers and labourers as they are to the better-known members of the gentry. Their names are known, but the work of the former is still there for us to see as the more important memorial.

Further reading

J.H. Bettey, *Estates and the English Countryside*, Batsford London 1993

James Bond & Kate Tiller (eds), *Blenheim: Landscape for a Palace*, Sutton Stroud 1987

Charles Saumarez Smith, *The Building of Castle Howard*, Pimlico London 1990

Anthea Taigel & Tom Williamson, *Parks and Gardens*, Batsford London 1993

Christopher Taylor, *Parks and Gardens of Britain: A Landscape History from the Air*, Edinburgh University Press 1998

Tom Williamson, *Polite Landscapes*, Sutton Stroud 1995

20

THE SOMERSET LEVELS

For the last section we return to Somerset to look at one of my favourite landscapes – the Somerset Levels. There is something about the flat, lowland, former marshy landscapes of this type of country that is very attractive, and the same is true of the other reclaimed lowland areas elsewhere. And yet with the single exception of the Norfolk Broads, none of them is a national park or afforded any of the statutory protection enjoyed by the areas of uplands of the country such the Lake District or Snowdonia. They tend to be areas that are not visited by tourists and walkers and are not popular as holiday destinations. It is as if an area has to be high and moorland to be thought to be attractive, interesting and worthy of protection. And yet these lowland areas show, almost more than any other, the efforts of generations of peasants and farmers in attempting to deal with flooding and trying to make the land productive and useful. Just because they are low lying and still usually subject to flooding, they have generally not been ploughed so that everything that has been done to them in the past is either still visible, because it is still in use, or remains as earth-

214 *Evidence of the peat digging activities in the Somerset Levels*

works as a clue to former activity. Recent studies of the wetlands of the Humber basin, the north-west lowlands of Cheshire and Lancashire, and particularly of the Fens of East Anglia and Romney Marsh in Sussex and Kent, show just how much interesting evidence of landscape development there is still remaining in these areas.

The Somerset Levels is a large area of low-lying land with peat and alluvium deposits between and around low upland areas and 'islands' in the centre of Somerset. The former peat bogs have been dug extensively in the past and the peat extracted for fuel and horticultural purposes (214). Away from the peat, the landscape has been comprehensively drained, at different times, to keep as much water off the land for as long as possible each year, and the grassland has been improved. The view in figure 215 shows the Greylake area right in the middle of the Levels with King's Sedgemoor off to the right. The present road is the successor to a medieval causeway built to link up the higher land of Sowy island to the left and the Polden Hills off to the right. The parallel channels are the Sowy River and the Langacre

Rhyne – rhyne being a local name for a drainage channel. An attempt had been made to drain this area in the seventeenth century but it was not until the late eighteenth century that this was achieved with the construction of King's Sedgemoor Drain by 1796 (**216**). Once it was drained the land could be enclosed with the pattern of regular rectangular fields that can be seen. The very dark peaty soil can be seen in the ploughed land in contrast to the lighter sandy soil of Sowy island (**215**).

During peat extraction (**217, 218**) many buried prehistoric timber structures have been found in these peat deposits; most of these are trackways and walkways of one

215 (Left) *Greylake and King's Sedgemoor with the Sowy River and Langacre Rhyne*

216 (Below left) *The reclaimed areas of the Levels near King's Sedgemoor Drain*

217 (Below) *Former areas of peat extraction at Shapwick; the Sweet Track ran across this area (between the arrows)*

218 *Flooded former peat extraction areas*

219 *The Bronze Age timber platform at Greylake under excavation*

sort or another. The views show the course of the Sweet Track dated, by dendrochronology, to 3807-3806 BC, and the areas of flooded worked-out peat beds near Meare. Elsewhere there are timber platforms and one of these was found near Greylake in 1997 (**219**) in excavations which produced human bones, probably indicating bodies had been exposed on the edge of the marsh.

In the Iron Age and through into the early Roman period a number of 'lake' villages existed on the margins of the Levels. Modern replicas of two of the houses from the Glastonbury lake village site have been erected at the Peat Moors Visitor Centre (**220**). There are also replicas of the trackways that have been found (and nearby the excellent café which kept us going with coffee and cake when working on the Shapwick project!).

Documented drainage and reclamation of the Levels dates from the Middle Ages onwards, with big campaigns

220 *The replica prehistoric houses at the Peat Moors Visitor Centre*

221 (Left) *The course of the River Tone near Athelney; this channel was dug in 1374-5 by Athelney Abbey and other local landowners*

222 (Above) *West Sedgemoor, drained in 1816, with its pattern of regular fields*

in the twelfth and thirteenth centuries by various ecclesiastical organizations (such as Glastonbury Abbey, the bishops of Bath and Wells) (**221**), and others in the seventeenth century and the eighteenth to nineteenth centuries. A good example of the latter is West Sedgemoor (**222**) which was drained in 1816 with the construction of a central rhyne and the North Drove rhyne seen in the photograph. Flooding on a large scale was not really eliminated in the central part of the Levels until the mid-twentieth century. This followed the digging of the Huntspill river in the 1940s (**223**). It was as if the Levels were a river short and the digging of this artificial river solved the problem!

It now seems likely that Roman engineers tried and probably succeeded in draining and managing the easier areas of the Levels such as the valley of the River Axe. Here there are extensive earthworks underlying the later

223 *The Huntspill river and the River Parrett in the background*

224 and **plan**
A complex of earthworks in the Axe valley, which seems to be the remains of Romano-British farmsteads sited on reclaimed land

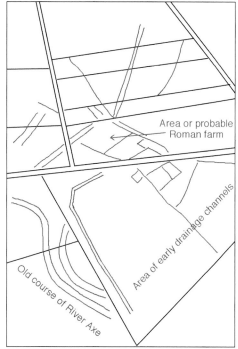

Area or probable Roman farm

Area of early drainage channels

Old course of River Axe

pattern of fields and some of the platforms of these have produced Roman pottery, quern stones and so on (**224**). They seem to have built canals and drained the land sufficiently for settlements to be established on the former floodable land, sometimes alongside earlier river courses that were presumably used for transport. These may only have been occupied seasonally of course, in the drier parts of the year (**225, 226**) and are most likely to have been stock farms running cattle on the rich grasslands.

227 *Glastonbury Tor – the tower of the church of St Michael marks the early monastery site*

225, 226 *Earthworks of the probable Roman canals built in the Axe valley*

In the centuries before the Norman Conquest, when the Levels were probably in their least managed state since prehistoric times, the islands sticking out of the marsh were popular with hermits and early ecclesiastical communities. The most famous is Glastonbury Tor (**227**) which seems to have been the site of a small monastery before

230 (Above) *The early site at Marchey*

231 (Below) *Oath, the site of a medieval hermitage in the Parrett valley*

228 (Above) *Muchelney – the 'big island'*

229 (Below) *The abbey at Muchelney*

the main site at Glastonbury Abbey was founded. But there are others at Muchelney (the 'big island') where there was a monastery from at least the seventh century (**228, 229**), Marchey (Martin's island) (**230**), Nyland Hill (Andresey – Andrew's island – see below) and possibly others like Oath (**231**) where there was a medieval hermitage and there might have been something earlier.

Vast areas of the Levels were owned by the Church in the Middle Ages and the resources brought from there were of immense importance. These included wood, timber and peat but also fish, especially eels, wildfowl, sedges and reeds. At Meare (**232**) there was a great lake (the 'mere' of the name) several miles across. Here the abbots of Glastonbury not only had a church and a manor house, which still survive, but also a fish house where the fishermen who worked on the lake stored their

233 *Bounds Ditch (the line between the arrows)*

232 *Meare, with its church, manor and fish house (right); in the background was the great lake, now reclaimed*

equipment and probably processed the fish. Next to this are medieval fishponds and the site of the medieval vineyard. There were frequent disputes about access to the resources of the Levels, the most famous occurring in 1326 when the men working for the abbot (of Glastonbury) and the bishop (of Bath and Wells) came to blows and a lot of destruction took place. It was agreed to divide the moors between Meare and Wedmore and a new dyke was cut and built marked by stone crosses. Bounds Ditch (**233**) follows the course of this boundary (and commemorates the dispute). The land of the bishops in Wedmore is in the foreground, that of the abbots in Meare in the background.

There are countless similar examples of what now appear to be insignificant banks and ditches in all the low-lying areas around the country. They may not look much but I think they are as important as the surviving documents and fine architecture of the period, and certainly they were of more significance to many of the people in the area at that time.

234 and **plan** *Nyland Hill and the Levels near Cheddar*

The final picture (**234**) brings us almost back to the beginning of this book. It shows the area south-west of Nyland Hill in Cheddar. The hill itself was called Andresey in earlier times, and was part of the earliest endowment of Glastonbury Abbey. The name probably meant Andrew's island, and it had a chapel and probably a monastery of hermits on the top in the pre-Norman period. It would have been surrounded by marshes although, as we have seen, some of this stretch of the Axe valley may have been drained and managed in the Roman period. The linear earthworks coming off the abandoned old river course of the Axe could in fact be Roman and relate to this phase of reclamation. At some stage before the seventeenth century the River Axe was put into a new straight course

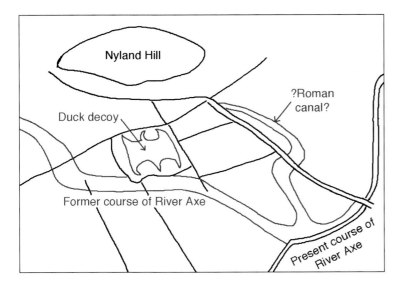

by digging a new channel for three or four miles through the valley. All over the fields there are drainage ditches dug to keep the fields free of water. Usually these have the same alignments as the field boundaries and so probably relate to that particular phase of enclosure (whenever it was). But occasionally ditches can be seen as earthworks on an altogether different orientation to these later field drains, and these channels must usually represent an earlier (or just possibly later) phase of drainage. By removing so much surface water from the fields for much of the year, some of the traditional activities of the Levels were inevitably severely disrupted.

These large areas of floodland always attracted lots of wildfowl and they were an important source of meat and feathers to early communities. Following drainage such areas shrunk in extent. In order to attract wildfowl and still be able to hunt them, artificial areas of water were developed together with the means to catch the birds. The resulting structure, the 'duck decoy', was developed and many were built in the Levels from the seventeenth century onwards. The characteristic square pool (now dry) with 'pipes', the channels coming off where the birds

were caught, and the surrounding ditch, can be seen near the centre of the picture.

In this one air view we can see so many aspects of how these lowland landscapes have been used and have developed over many centuries, in this case from the evidence of earthworks and from the patterns and alignments of structures and boundaries still there in the countryside. In many senses this bit of landscape near Cheddar can stand as a microcosm for all the other examples in this book. These landscapes are monuments to the, usually ordinary, earlier people who have worked in and created them, transforming wild natural countryside into agricultural and urban landscapes, by clearing woodland and waste, digging ditches, draining marshes and putting in hedges, which would then provide the sustenance they needed. Much of the best evidence, which can be used to build up the story of how this took place, such as earthworks and cropmarks, can only really be appreciated from the air. Aerial reconnaissance, the aerial view and the air photographs can be seen therefore to be one of the prime research methods (along with fieldwork, documents, geophysical survey and so on) for understanding much of how different landscapes have developed over the last few millennia. I hope the examples chosen and illustrated in this book have demonstrated this point of view to the full.

Further reading

Bryony & John Coles, *Sweet Track to Glastonbury: The Somerset Levels in Prehistory*, Thames and Hudson 1986

Jill Eddison, *Romney Marsh: Survival on a Frontier*, Tempus Stroud 2000

David Hall & John Coles, *Fenland Survey: An Essay in Landscape and Persistence*, English Heritage 1994

Stephen Rippon, *The Severn Estuary: Landscape Evolution and Wetland Reclamation*, Leicester University Press 1997

Michael Williams, *The Draining of the Somerset Levels*, Cambridge University Press 1970

GENERAL BIBLIOGRAPHY, REFERENCES & FURTHER READING

In this brief bibliography I have included almost everything in book form that has been written about aerial survey in archaeology. Many of the books include selections of superb air photographs of sites in their landscapes. I have also included general material of relevance to many of the sections in this book such as the Pevsner volumes about the buildings in each county. As a number of sections here are about Somerset I have included rather more on that county than any others. Recently there has been a vogue for publishing collections of air photos for particular counties. I have included those I know about; I have no doubt there are others I have missed. I would be grateful to hear of any others so that I can include them in future editions of this book.

I have not attempted to provide a full bibliography for books on landscape archaeology. The seminal work was William Hoskins, *Making of the English Landscape*, published in 1955 by Hodder and Stoughton. The 1988 edition with extensive notes and comments by Christopher Taylor gives a better reflection of current views. Apart from my own *Interpreting the Landscape* (latest edition Routledge 1997) readers should consult any books by Maurice Beresford, Christopher Taylor, Richard Muir, Trevor Rowley, Oliver Rackham and Tom Williamson.

Mick Aston (ed.), *Aspects of the Medieval Landscape of Somerset*, Somerset County Council 1988

Mick Aston & Ian Burrow (eds), *The Archaeology of Somerset*, Somerset County Council 1982

M.W. Beresford & J.K.S. St Joseph, *Medieval England: An Aerial Survey*, Cambridge University Press 1958 and 1979

R. Allen Brown, *Castles from the Air*, Cambridge University Press 1989

Christopher Chaplin, *Dorset from the Air*, Dovecote Press Wimborne Dorset 1985

O.G.S. Crawford & A. Keiller, *Wessex from the Air*, Oxford 1928

Robert Croft & Mick Aston, *Somerset from the Air*, Somerset County Council 1993

Timothy Darvill, *Prehistoric Britain from the Air: A Study of Space, Time and Society*, Cambridge University Press 1996

Derek A. Edwards & Peter Wade-Martins, *Norfolk from the Air*, Norfolk Museums Service 1987

S.S. Frere & J.K.S. St Joseph, *Roman Britain from the Air*, Cambridge University Press 1983

Robin Glasscock (ed.), *Historic Landscapes of Britain from the Air*, Cambridge University Press 1992

Frances Griffith, *Devon's Past: An Aerial View*, Devon Books Exeter 1988

Kenneth Hudson, *Industrial History from the Air*, Cambridge University Press 1984

David Knowles & J.K.S. St Joseph, *Monastic Sites from the Air*, Cambridge University Press 1952

G.S. Maxwell (ed.), *The Impact of Aerial Reconnaissance on Archaeology*, Council for British Archaeology Research Report 49 1983

Richard Muir, *History from the Air*, Michael Joseph London 1983

Chris Musson, *Wales from the Air: Patterns of Past and Present*, Royal Commission on the Ancient and Historical Monuments of Wales Aberystwyth 1994

Susan Oosthuizen, *Cambridgeshire from the Air*, Sutton Stroud 1996

Nicholas Pevsner, *Buildings of England* series for individual counties published by Penguin

Claire Pinder, Steve Wallis & Laurence Keen, *Dorset from the Air*, Dorset Books Tiverton Devon 1998

Colin Platt, *Medieval Britain from the Air*, Guild London 1984

D.N. Riley, *Early Landscapes from the Air: Studies of Cropmarks in South Yorkshire and North Nottinghamshire*, University of Sheffield 1980

D.N. Riley, *Air Photography and Archaeology*, Duckworth London 1987

Christopher Stanley, *The History of Britain: An Aerial View*, Batsford London 1984

David Strachan, *Essex from the Air: Archaeology and History from Aerial Photographs*, Essex County Council 1998

J.K.S. St Joseph (ed.), *The Uses of Air Photography*, John Baker London 1966 and 1977

Christopher Taylor, *Parks and Gardens of Britain: A Landscape History from the Air*, Edinburgh University Press 1998

Michael Watson & Chris Musson, *Shropshire from the Air*, Shropshire Books 1993

David Wilson, *Air Photo Interpretation for Archaeologists*, Tempus Stroud 2000

D.R. Wilson (ed.), *Aerial Reconnaissance for Archaeology*, Council for British Archaeology Research Report 12 1975

INDEX

Page numbers in **bold** refer to illustrations